The

Ornament

of a

Spirit

Exploring the Reasons
Covering Styles Change

Cory A. Anderson

Ridgeway Publishing
Stoneboro, PA 16153

THE ORNAMENT OF A SPIRIT

To order additional copies,
please visit your local
bookstore or contact:

Ridgeway Publishing
2080 McComb Rd.
Stoneboro, PA 16153
ph: 888.822.7894
fax: 585.798.9016

Cover design by: M. Gagarin Design

ISBN# 978-0-984-0984-1-4

Table of Contents

Preface

A t the time of publication for this second edition, it has only been just under three years since the first edition of *Ornament of a Spirit* was released. Yet, during this brief interlude, conservative Anabaptist churches have faced a barrage of changes and questions about head covering styles; several churches have even implemented permanent, sweeping alterations to their head coverings. More people are seeking answers to this hotly contested debate that so lacks clarity, and the issue continues to intensify. The response to this book has been largely positive among the readership. Varied as a more cross-sectional response may be, one thing is evident: that this topic saturates the marrow of conservative Anabaptist bones. People are passionate about this issue on all sides. Feedback to the first edition made me realize that certain areas of the book require clarification, while other areas would benefit from expansion.

Part I of this book, addressing the doctrine of the head covering, remains virtually unchanged. Consensus on this material was easily acquired. That said, our belief in a doctrine is only as good as our practice. The manifestation of an abstract doctrine is, without surprise, the domain of the most intense discussion and need for clarity.

Accordingly, several chapters in Part II have been reworked, reorganized, and revised. Readers have latched onto the concept of head covering symbolism. The resulting discussions and questions raised suggested a need for reworking this material, and I hope it has now reached a higher standard of clarity. This incorporates new material developed from presentations at the March 2011 Anabaptist Identity Conference, invited talks at conservative churches, and consultation with a fashion designer over elements of covering style. Chapters five and six on symbolism and motivations, respectively, have been swapped in order. Chapters four and seven, focusing on how churches now and in the past have executed this doctrine, have remained basically the same, but my wife and I anticipate expanding awareness of these issues in a forthcoming publication. Chapter nine, addressing tangible issues, has also been considerably reworked for clarity and depth of discussion.

Finally, this book includes two new appendices. The first attempts to capture the numerous miniature "nugget" questions and statements on this topic. The goal is to, in turn, respond with such a "nugget." Its intended use is for quick reference. The second appendix provides basic instructions for women on care for their cap-style coverings. Finally, the popular head covering photo index has been expanded. Several low-quality photos have also been replaced. It is my prayer that the reader is blessed with a deeper commitment to Christianity and our churches through this project.

— Cory Anderson

Acknowledgments

Prom a self-reflective collection of thoughts to a position paper distributed to friends and eventually to its current form in a book, this document bears the colorful stamp of several people. Steven Kooistra of Indiana contributed substantially to Section II, both in editing my portions and in contributing portions of his own writing. His close involvement was invaluable and his perspectives were indispensable. Thank you, Steve, for your insight and friendship. I also extend my gratitude to Greg Rich of Kentucky for taking a supportive interest in this project and encouraging its development to what it is now. Further, I acknowledge the input of many who read the manuscript and offered constructive criticism.

Though I present cases in favor of the traditional covering, I have friends who have chosen a veil style. They, like many others in the Christian family, have blessed my life richly in diverse ways. I wish to affirm those friendships. Numerous authors are quoted in this book, from ancient writers to contemporary church leaders to secular thinkers. A quotation from an author does not necessarily indicate his endorsement of the views in this work.

Introduction and
Historical Background

Few New Testament teachings are as clearly taught and yet flatly refused by modern Western Christians as the woman's head covering. Paul reminded the Corinthians of this eternal principle in 1 Corinthians 11:1-16, the source of the clearest teaching about this doctrine. While observed by Christian—and even pagan—society throughout most of history, the practice largely disappeared during the 1920s.

During this decade a cultural revolution of new ideas, technology, and prosperity thrust Americans into a fantasy world of heroes, unrealistic romances, and fleeting thrills sought from the world in moving picture shows, immoral parties, wild dancing to sensual music, beachside beauty contests, radio programs, sports idols, movie stars, amusement parks, and a constant bombardment of subtly deceptive advertisements stimulating consumerism.

These diversions taught Americans that the Victorian era of the 1800s and early 1900s was oppressive and that any who held to the moral and social conduct of that time were "Puritans," a historically inaccurate portrayal of hypocritical, stern, religious people who suppressed their own carnal desires. Young people who used the term "Puritan" looked to peers instead of parents for moral standards. They quoted Sigmund

Freud, though they knew little about psychology, clinging to the theory that mankind needs to cast off restraint and indulge his base human drives, especially those leading to aggression and impurity.

This attack on the values of earlier generations succeeded and, ever since, society has spiraled downward, pursuing a never-ending, never-satisfying lifestyle of pleasure and immediate gratification. Among the many symbols of the past "oppressive" era was the woman's religious head covering. Conservative Christian women wore hats to church for a few decades after that, but the bonnet and cap styles were largely discarded.

Several denominations in the 1920s sought to reinforce the doctrine of the head covering. Of the more visible efforts, leaders of the (Old) Mennonite Church such as George R. Brunk Sr. and Daniel Kauffman helped save the covering from being seen merely as a Victorian-era cultural nuance subject to change with fashion. Thousands of Anabaptist women, guided by strong leadership, purposefully continued to don the head covering during this time. However, an undercurrent of resistance chipped away at the conviction and practice. In the decades after World War II, some Mennonite constituencies dropped the practice, as well as other distinguishing practices and doctrines. Despite this loss, many others have remained faithful to the doctrine.

May this book assist its readers in understanding the eternal principles expressed in the practice of the head covering. May the reader take to heart a consuming Christian zeal (John 2:17). May it help the reader stand firmly on the foundation of Jesus Christ and not on the rubble of society's reasoning.

For other foundation can no man lay than that is laid, which is Jesus Christ. Now if any man build upon this foundation gold, silver, precious stones, wood, hay, stubble; every man's work shall be made manifest: for the day shall declare it, because it shall be revealed by fire; and the fire shall try every man's work of what sort it is. (1 Corinthians 3:11-13)

This book is divided into two sections. Section I analyzes 1 Corinthians 11:1-16 in order to understand the reasons for the Christian woman's head covering. It also discusses scriptural direction as to how often and where women are to cover. The section then addresses seven common criticisms of 1 Corinthians 11:1-16. In Section I, "covering" and "veil" are used interchangeably.

Section II demonstrates how the same worldly spirit that is against the wearing of the covering is making its way into Anabaptist churches in the form of covering style changes. These changes are often from a traditional style, such as the pleated cap, to the hanging veil and its abbreviated cousins. This section will probe some of the varying motivations behind the changes as well as positive and negative attributes of the changing styles.

Section I

The Doctrine of the
Head Covering

A Discussion of
1 Corinthians 11:1-16

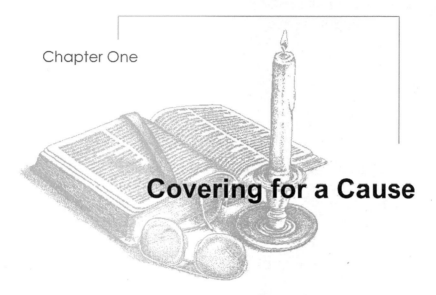

Chapter One

Covering for a Cause

I n his first letter to the Corinthians, Paul spells out some of the clearest guides to practical holy living of all his writings. It is not for a lack of clarity that his guidance is misconstrued or rejected. Already, while Paul perhaps still lived, Peter writes that "they that are unlearned and unstable wrest [Paul's epistles], as they do also the other Scriptures, unto their own destruction" (2 Peter 3:16).

Among the clear teachings so often victimized is the woman's head covering discussed in 1 Corinthians 11:1-16. This chapter will review what this passage and other Scriptures say about the covering. In addition, this chapter will discuss further justifications for the covering extending beyond Scripture into what Paul calls "nature" (1 Corinthians 11:14). Despite the clarity of Paul's teaching, this section of Scripture leaves many mysteries for the believer to discover, and this chapter will probe some of the possibilities to enrich the discussion and prompt the reader to ponder the mysteries of this practice. While others have written more extensively on the doctrine of the head covering,[1] this first section is intended to provide a shorter discussion about the meaning and purpose of the teaching.

1) In Recognition of the Headship Order

Paul explained the headship order in 1 Corinthians 11:3: God⇒Christ⇒Man⇒Woman. This order is grounded in Creation (11:8-9). In the beginning was God (Genesis 1:1). And the Word (Christ) was with God, and the Word was God. Christ submits to His Father and seeks to honor Him (John 5:19, 23, 26-30). Only through Christ does mankind have access to God (John 6:44; 14:6; Acts 4:12). God created man in His image, then created woman in His image from the flesh of man to be a help to him (Genesis 2:18, 21-23; 1 Timothy 2:13; 1 Corinthians 11:7).

What qualities of headship does Paul specifically discuss in the 1 Corinthians 11:1-16 passage? He mentions two: the potential to be a "glory" (11:7) or a "dishonor" (11:4-5) to a head. A woman, specifically, may find it a "shame" to go without a covering (11:6). Headship is a position of responsibility, of love and care, of humble deference to bring glory and honor to our respective heads, be it mankind, Christ, or God. For a woman to wear the covering identifies her position as the glory of man (v. 7), demonstrates her desire to honor man (v. 5), and enables her to avoid shame (v. 6).

Paul does not discuss the biblical concept of submission in

---

[1] Many such works are cited throughout this book and in the bibliography.

the context of the head covering. Christian women who wear the covering often wrestle with the question: Do I have to do whatever any man tells me if I am in submission to mankind? Though submission is a biblical concept within certain God-ordained relationships, Paul does not explicitly mention submission as a principle of the head covering in 1 Corinthians 11:1-16. Therefore, Paul could speak of mankind and womankind generally.[2] If he spoke of submission, he would have had to refer to a specific relationship between a man and woman, such as father-daughter or husband-wife. Otherwise, he would be saying all women must do whatever any man says.

Perhaps Paul was *implying* the concept of submission with the covering, or perhaps he embedded the concept of submission into his use of the term "head." But without speculating, we can only conclude that Paul did not mention it directly in this chapter. Conversely, neither can we say definitely that submission is excluded from this practice.

Perhaps an investigation of the passages about submission could reveal more clues about the point Paul was making in 1 Corinthians 11. Interestingly, in the two epistles where Paul teaches headship as an expression of submission, he does not speak of mankind and womankind. He speaks rather of specific relationships: husband-wife, parents-children, and Christ-church (Ephesians 5:22-25, 6:1-4; Colossians 3:18-22). These are three headship order models different from the model in 1 Corinthians 11, God⇒Christ⇒mankind⇒womankind. In Ephesians and Colossians, he does not speak of the head covering,

---

[2] Several Bible translations, such as the ESV, erroneously translate "man" and "woman" as "husband" and "wife" in 1 Corinthians 11. However, the vast majority of translations are faithful to the original text. Tertullian, an early church writer, argued in Chapter 3 of On the *Veiling of Virgins* that the commandment applies just as much to the unmarried as to the married because the issues of headship, angels, and modesty apply to all women.

"glory," or "dishonor," but commands submission, love, and obedience as principles in themselves within these three orders. The headship order of Creation discussed in Corinthians and the headship order of relationships in Ephesians and Colossians are certainly not exclusive of or contradictory to one another, but they are slightly different teachings.

The analogy of a "head" in 1 Corinthians 11:1-16 and a "body" such as in 1 Corinthians 12 is inspiring. Paul used the illustration of a physical head to describe headship and a physical body to describe the mechanism of glory for the head. In human anatomy, the head decides what to do and the body does it. If God is the head of Christ, then perhaps Christ is the body of God that labors for Him. If Christ is the head of man, then men fulfill their headship role to Christ when they function as Christ's body, working for Him and thereby glorifying Him. Men may therefore be assured that they are in their proper headship role when they bring glory to Christ through their lives.

Mankind is the head of womankind, so the analogy may follow that women glorify men when they serve as the body of men, laboring to support men's labor for Christ as He serves God. Thus, women indirectly bring glory to Christ by assisting men in bringing glory to Christ. Women also have opportunity to participate directly in the salvation of Christ through their role in the Church, as mentioned in the headship order of Christ⇒Church in Ephesians 5:23, for Christ "is the Saviour of the body."

The symbol of this headship order is the covering. Beyond 1 Corinthians 11, other passages in the Bible describe a head covering. Under the Old Covenant, male leaders such as Moses also wore a covering of religious significance.

> But when Moses went in before the LORD to
> speak with him, he took the vail off, until he
> came out. And he came out, and spake unto the
> children of Israel that which he was commanded.
> And the children of Israel saw the face of Moses,
> that the skin of Moses' face shone: and Moses put
> the vail upon his face again, until he went in to
> speak with [God]. (Exodus 34:34-35)

Paul further explained why Moses veiled himself.

> And not as Moses, which put a vail over his face,
> that the children of Israel could not steadfastly
> look to the end of that which is abolished: but
> their minds were blinded: for until this day re-
> maineth the same vail untaken away in the read-
> ing of the old testament; which vail is done away
> in Christ. (2 Corinthians 3:13-14)

Paul acknowledges a practical reason why Moses wore a covering, because of the brightness of his face. However, Paul does not rest the case there, but presents an analogy and figurative meaning for Moses' covering, much as he also describes a figurative meaning of the women's covering in 1 Corinthians 11.

Most of the reasons Moses and other Jewish men covered their heads remain a mystery, but some speculation on the subject might help us understand part of the larger mystery of head covering usage throughout time. Perhaps Moses, certain Levites, and other figures in the community wore the veil as a symbolic covering of the Christ who was yet to come. We know Moses removed it when in the presence of the Lord, as he was in the immediate presence of and had direct access to God. "And the Lord spake unto Moses, as a man speaketh unto his friends" (Exodus 33:11). According to the order of headship in

1 Corinthians 11:3, Christ is between man and God: God, then Christ, then man, then woman. Since Christ had yet to offer Himself as a sacrifice and since God did not appear to others with the physical presence He appeared to Moses, the appointed men may have worn a covering to "cover" their spiritual head, Christ, until the time Christ would come, and the Spirit of God would intimately rest within believers, for the "vail is done away with in Christ."

Presently, Christ is the intercessor in prayer between men and God (Romans 8:34; Hebrews 7:25), so this could explain why a covering for men is no longer needed. It may be that men no longer need to cover their heads in anticipation of the Saviour's arrival. That is perhaps why Paul said in 1 Corinthians 11:4, "Every man praying or prophesying, having his head covered, dishonoureth his head." Since Christ has come and made His sacrifice, it would be an offense to Jesus' death for a man to cover his "head" as practiced under the Law because the man is symbolically covering the revealed Christ.

Conservative Jewish men still cover their heads today. They do this out of recognition of God above them, as described in the Talmud[3] (Shabbat 156b). The teaching predates the New Testament, demonstrating that Jewish men wore a covering of religious significance before Paul's teaching. While many then and now wear it at all times, it is especially important to wear while walking somewhere (Shulchan Aruch 2:6), in prayer, during worship, and during meals. The practice was reinforced, ironically, by Jews wanting to distinguish themselves from European Christian men in the 1500s, who removed their coverings to show respect for God.[4]

The Jews continued the practice after Christ, but Paul found it neces-

---

[3] The Talmud is a collection of the Jewish oral law and commentary, formed and compiled in the centuries after the destruction of the temple in A.D. 70.
[4] "Wearing a Yarmulka," published by KOF-K: Kosher Supervision, Teaneck, NJ.

sary to clarify the appropriate practice in light of Christ's appearance. The church evidently knew the traditions and practiced them faithfully, as Paul acknowledged in 1 Corinthians 11:2: "Now I praise you, brethren, that ye remember me in all things, and keep the ordinances, as I delivered them to you." Just as Christians today may have lost understanding of certain practices, perhaps the Corinthians did not remember the historical significance of head coverings for men and women. Therefore, they may not have realized that Christ's resurrection necessitated a change in this practice.

Beyond the symbolic meaning behind covering one's head, Paul clearly differentiates between the genders by assigning different practices for men and women. Acknowledging separate roles for each gender is critical for the headship order. In this age, there is much confusion about gender roles. Many rebel against this headship order. It is now acceptable in most professing Christian churches for women to assume leadership roles. Sometime after writing the Epistle to the Corinthians, Paul wrote to Timothy, saying,

> But I suffer not a woman to teach, nor to usurp authority over the man, but to be in silence. For Adam was first formed, then Eve. And Adam was not deceived, but the woman being deceived was in the transgression. (1 Timothy 2:12-14)

A covered head is a sign that a woman acknowledges where God has placed her in life. She accepts all the roles of women: the grave and sober wife (1 Timothy 3:11), the mother and grandmother (2 Timothy 1:5), the faithfully unmarried (1 Corinthians 7:34), the teacher of good things (Titus 2:3-5), an encouraging widow (1 Timothy 5:5-10), and a spiritual mother or sister (1 Timothy 5:2). She is joyful in the roles that God has given her for the furthering of the kingdom.

God knows how each soul should be placed in life to maximize that individual's talents. Men must take the initiative to fill the roles they have been given and to be Christian leaders rather than avoiding responsibility in the church, at home, or in any calling. The covering shows woman's support of man's activities. So that men do not abuse this position, Paul wrote, "Nevertheless neither is the man without the woman, neither the woman without the man, in the Lord" (1 Corinthians 11:11). True, God made woman from man in the beginning, but all men, including Christ, have since come from women.

2) Because of the Angels

"For this cause ought the woman to have power on her head because of the angels" (1 Corinthians 11:10). Paul chose not to elaborate further about this subject, leaving much about which to speculate. Even if a definitive conclusion is unreachable, it should not keep Christians from receiving the hidden blessings seen through this window. The mere instruction that the covering should be worn "because of the angels" should be enough to accept in faith.

To understand the angels' relationship with the head covering, one must investigate the broader role of angels. In the New Testament, angels were often involved with prayer.

> And [Zacharias and his wife Elisabeth] were both righteous before God, walking in all the commandments and ordinances of the Lord blameless. And they had no child. ... And there appeared unto him an angel. ... The angel said unto him, Fear not, Zacharias: for thy prayer is heard; and thy wife Elisabeth shall bear thee a son, and thou shalt call his name John. (Luke 1:6-7, 11, 13)

Both Zacharias and Elisabeth were righteous and obedient to the Lord's commands. Then, after they had been faithful, God answered their prayers. The Lord chose the angel Gabriel to deliver a message in response to their prayer.

John also spoke of how angels handle the prayers of God's people.

> And another angel came and stood at the altar, having a golden censer; and there was given unto him much incense, that he should offer it with the prayers of all saints upon the golden altar which was before the throne. (Revelation 8:3)

In this passage, an angel added incense to the prayers, making them more delightful to God. If wearing a covering is going to help the angels to somehow handle the prayers and deliver them to God, that alone is reason enough to wear one. The Amplified Bible mentions that one does not want to "displease" the angels by not wearing a covering. The meaningfulness of the intercession of angels may strike the wearer more powerfully to realize that in the chapters surrounding 1 Corinthians 11, Paul is speaking not just about the daily Christian life, but he is highlighting the teachings within the context of church services. The ordered presence of the saints in a church service with women's heads covered is certainly an environment in which the angels may assist men and women in worshiping God.

Angels are also charged with protection.

> And when Peter was come to himself, he said, Now I know of a surety, that the Lord hath sent his angel, and hath delivered me out of the hand of Herod, and from all the expectation of the people of the Jews. (Acts 12:11)

There are also angels that have rebelled against God. It may be that the covering is a sign for these angels too—a sign of protection from wickedness. A primary reference about the Jewish men's head covering in the Talmud develops this theme. Astrologers told a boy's mother that he would be a thief, but his mother commanded him to cover so that the fear of heaven would be upon him, and so that he could pray for mercy. Many personal testimonies of women today attribute their protection and safety from others who would do them harm to the wearing of a head covering.

3) Modesty

Though not specifically taught in 1 Corinthians 11, the Bible, as well as "nature," demonstrates that a head covering must be worn out of modesty. This is recognized by cultures all over the world today, as well as Jewish texts from ancient Israel: "The watchmen that went about the city found me, they smote me, they wounded me; the keepers of the walls took away my veil from me" (Song of Solomon 5:7). The watchmen added insult to injury, forcibly unveiling the woman. Women were to have a proper shame of being unveiled in the company of others. Another ancient text showing evidence of this concept is from the Old Testament Apocryphal account of Susanna. Two elders take Susanna to court and falsely accuse her of adultery after she refuses their approaches.

> Now Susanna was a very delicate woman and beauteous to behold. And these wicked men commanded to uncover her face [or "ordered her to be unveiled" in the NRSV] (for she was covered) that they might be filled with her beauty. There-

fore her friends, and all that saw her, wept.
(Susanna 31-33, KJV)

Whether or not the account is historically accurate, it reveals a period view of Jewish beliefs about modesty and the covering. The veil Susanna wore was used to reserve her beauty. She maintained this reserve when she went to be judged. To have her veil removed was to her shame and exposure. The elders knew this was a public statement of shame and used it to cover their lustful intentions.

This story is not an isolated example. For a wife especially to have her hair covered has long been a Jewish practice of modesty, as affirmed by bodies of ancient and more contemporary Jewish literature. This includes the Talmud, which refers to going out uncovered as a violation of Jewish practice worthy of divorce.[5] Thus Judaism, from which Christianity emerged, recognized the covering for women as an issue of modesty, and this was likely acknowledged by the early Christians.

In Western society, it was not until the 1920s that women let their hair down and cut it, a reflection of the sensual direction popular culture was taking. Other groups around the world acknowledge the attraction of women's hair. Muslim men and women, for example, wear coverings because, among other reasons, of the attention that less restrictive cultures like the West give to the hair in developing an imposing personal display. Sikh women wear turbans like the men for identity, but women wear an additional covering over the religious turban to signify modesty and reserve.

Covering the hair for the sake of modesty does not appear

---

[5] For a thorough discussion of Jewish literature about the woman's head covering, see Rabbi Mayer Schiller's article "The Obligation of Married Women to Cover Their Hair" in the Journal of Halacha, Vol. 30, pp. 81-108, 1995.

to be isolated to one ethnic group or one religion. It appears to be something taught by nature to people around the world. Like all women, a Christian woman today must conceal her hair in a covering as a way to reserve the beauty God has given to women.

4) Outward Testimony: "Why do you wear that thing on your head?"

Because the woman's veil is no longer commonly practiced in Western society, observers may wonder about the unusual article and even inquire about its purpose. Without a good grasp of the covering's significance, a woman may lose an opportunity to bless someone or may mislead the inquirer. The answer may be apologetic: "Because my church makes me." It may be unlearned: "We're Mennonites/Amish, and that's what we do."[6] It may be embarrassing: "I'm not really sure why; we've just always done it."[7] But to the woman who is confident in her reasons for covering, a clear answer is an open door to share this biblical practice with other professing Christians or to lead into deeper conversations with non-Christians, prompting them to reconsider the sovereignty of God.

During the early twentieth century, the Christian church largely dropped the practice of women covering. Today, when a woman from a church that does not practice this doctrine starts covering her head consistently, others in her church may wonder why, providing an opportunity to share. Unfortunately, churches too often reject the woman who begins covering. The

---

[6] This answer is not bad in itself, but lacks a link to Scripture. A member's willingness to associate and identify with her Anabaptist denomination is healthy and appeals to the fact that this is a practice observed not just by an individual. People outside Anabaptist circles often notice Amish and Mennonite head coverings, identifying the women by that symbol.

[7] Pointing out the endurance of a practice over many generations is a good testimony, but again, a link to Scripture furthers the case.

symbol becomes a threat to others. Such strong opposition to a seemingly minor change, though unfortunate, testifies to the truth of the doctrine.

Non-Christian acquaintances may also want to know why a woman is wearing a covering. Here is another opportunity to describe the faith she has in the salvation of Christ and the nature of His commands. The covering provides non-Christians with a visible testimony to her devoutness in the faith and shows that she is willing to stand apart from society to follow the Bible. What a great testimony of true Christian zeal in a culture of lukewarm Christians!

Consider these reports from five women who began wearing the head covering. Notice the responses from churches, families, and employers:

> This is my first week wearing the covering consistently, which for me was a large step in overcoming the fear of man's opinion. I did run into a bit of an issue at work yesterday when my boss asked me to remove the covering. We had a meeting and I explained its purpose. She seems okay for the moment. I have prayed about 1 Corinthians 11 for about four years now. I suppose the most convincing piece of evidence for the covering is the absolute opposition to it from the world. I do have the support of one of my brothers. I really hadn't expected him to be interested, but he actually wants to visit the church with me sometime.

> I have taken on the head covering and plain dress for myself but find that this calling can sometimes be lonely.

> As I studied about the Christian woman's veiling, feet washing, and nonresistance, I wondered why

these things were missing from all that preaching I sat through years ago. As I told my husband, I felt as though I had been in a spiritual coma for years. Of course he noticed that I was dressing differently and wearing a head covering, so we have had many conversations about spiritual things, and he is interested to learn more.

When I came to the church [non-Anabaptist], only about half of the women covered during the service, and few covered all the time. More recently, after we had been focusing on biblical teachings regarding the home and the roles of husbands and wives, many more women have been convicted about this and have begun to cover, some during the service and some all the time. Others are beginning to wear skirts or dresses exclusively and have been convicted in other areas as well.

At a Bible study, the church handed out a paper about the covering, but none of the verses match what my Bible says. The paper says that if a woman covers, it results in: deception (1 Timothy 2:13,14); moral impurity (Genesis 34:1-2); breakdown of family relationships (Genesis 27:5-13); barrenness (2 Samuel 6:20-23); confusion (1 Corinthians 14:34, 35); manipulation (dominating spirit) (1 Kings 21:4-7); and prevention of husband's possible salvation (1 Peter 3:1). Belonging to a church that says this about the covering has me in tears.

I feel convicted to really learn the Bible and do what God wants for my life. While studying I read about the headcovering. This made me wonder why the [...] church I was attending didn't practice this. Why didn't any church I had attended? I spoke to women in the church about why and they didn't know. So, I started headcovering and received no support. I felt rejected. We visited a [...] church that my kids like. It's ok to wear hats but they also don't teach plain dress or headcovering. Online research that I've done has only made me more convicted. I really want to obey God and find others that would be supportive. I would love to find a church that will guide me to a closer relationship to Christ and follow his word.

Those of us who recognize the truth of this doctrine and choose to observe the Christian woman's head covering need to bear in mind the responsibility that accompanies this honor and make sure our words and actions bear witness to the godly testimony of the veil. There is an account in the Old Testament of women abusing this trusted symbol and using it deceptively to ensnare naïve people with evil.

Wherefore thus saith the Lord God; Behold, I am against your pillows [and charms and veils— Amplified] wherewith ye there hunt the souls to make them fly, and I will tear them from your arms, and will let the souls go, even the souls that ye hunt to make them fly. Your kerchiefs [deceptive veils—Amplified] also will I tear, and deliver my people out of your hand ... because with lies ye have made the heart of the righteous sad, whom I have not made sad; and strengthened the hands of the wicked, that he should not return from his wicked way, by promising him life. (Ezekiel 13:20-22)

Christian women who cover have a responsibility to be consistent. People are watching. Unlike the women who hunted for souls, Christian women use their veils as a beacon to other

Christians. A woman who covers and appears to be a person of conviction is quickly trusted, whether with watching over personal belongings or as a listening ear.

The Christian woman needs to lift up the souls of the sad, strengthen the hearts of the righteous, and encourage others to follow the true path toward the Lord. This implies that women who wear coverings in righteousness and obedience should uphold the blessed attributes that covering represents. Let it not become a symbol of mistrust to the world through carelessness and inconsistency in behavior and activities.

The covering is an encouragement to other devout Christians. It is beautiful to enter into a gathering of Christians prepared to worship God and see reverently covered heads. When one Christian woman who covers sees another veiled Christian woman in an unlikely place, there is an immediate bond.

Professing Christians who copy society's fashions miss this blessing. Protestant Christians who do not cover or who disagree with the doctrine are often blessed by the commitment and zeal demonstrated by Christian churches that persevere in this doctrine, because it takes devotion and self-denial in today's society to practice something that sets one apart.

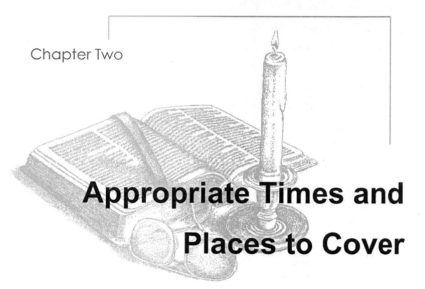

Chapter Two

Appropriate Times and
Places to Cover

T he Bible exhorts women to give attention to covering
when in the act of praying or prophesying. "But every woman that prayeth or prophesieth with her head uncovered dishonoureth her head: for that is even all one as if she were
shaven" (1 Corinthians 11:5). Scriptural principles and the actual practice of the Corinthians would indicate God's intention
for the covering to be worn at all times, not just during times of
direct communication with God.

While Paul had the assembly of saints in mind when he
wrote, the principles of covering apply to all times of the believer's life, not only church services. The testimony of headship
and the angels applies just as much in private as in public.
Therefore, women must be conscientious in wearing the covering during private or family devotions.

How often does a woman pray? Where does she pray? The

New Testament reminds the believer to pray often, even continually (Acts 6:3-4,6; 12:5; Romans 1:8-10; Ephesians 1:15-19; 6:18-20; Colossians 1:3-4; 5:17; 2 Timothy 1:3-6). Perhaps most familiar is the succinct admonition of 1 Thessalonians 5:17: "Pray without ceasing." Believers are to maintain continual connection to God in their spirits, seeking His direction constantly, living in a state of prayer. Despite this, it seems reasonable to make allowance for times of being uncovered, such as for hygiene or to show her husband her hair. But God rejoices in the woman who desires to please Him by consistently praying and therefore consistently covering.

When kneeling or prostrating oneself in deliberate prayer, a covered head is a necessity. The wearing of the covering serves as a reminder to devote time to specific, direct prayer throughout the day. The opportunities and times to pray are numerous. The New Testament examples point to diverse times of prayer, including:

Before morning (Mark 1:35)

Around noon (sixth hour) (Acts 10:9)

In the late afternoon into evening (ninth hour) (Matthew 14:23; Acts 10:2-4)

At midnight (Acts 16:25)

Night and day (1 Thessalonians 3:9-10; 2 Timothy 1:3-6)

On the Sabbath and routinely with others (Acts 16:13-16)

During times of dire need (Acts 12:5)

Upon every remembrance of the faithful (Philippians 1:3-7; 2 Timothy 1:3-6)

After hearing a good report of someone in the faith (Ephesians 1:15-19; Colossians 1:3-4)

Prophesying may receive less attention, as it is not as familiar a practice to Christians today. The revelations of Old Testament prophets seem foreign to our present church situation, but God used women in this way, as recorded in Exodus 15:20, Judges 4:4, and Luke 2:36. First Corinthians 14:3 defines a more familiar prophesying for churches today: "But he that prophesieth speaketh unto men to edification, and exhortation, and comfort." The Amplified Bible offers a helpful clarification of a Christian woman's role in prophesying in 1 Corinthians 11:5: "teaches, refutes, admonishes, or comforts." There are appropriate times for women to do all these things.

In 1 Corinthians 14:34-35, while speaking about orderly prophesying in church services, Paul commands women to remain silent. It seems, then, that Paul expected women to prophesy at some time, just not in church services. Thus, Paul expected the covering to be worn more often than just for services. Women are therefore to wear the covering not only when they pray, whether at church or otherwise, but also whenever they engage in spiritual responsibility beyond the church service. As a Christian woman's responsibilities are ongoing, a woman should accustom herself to being covered throughout the day.

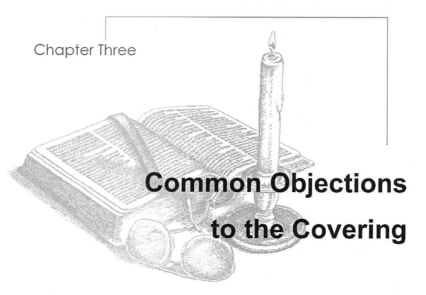

Chapter Three

Common Objections to the Covering

As long as there has been a Bible, there have been people who misinterpret passages to say what they want them to say. The root spirit says, "I need to conform the Bible to my lifestyle," instead of, "I need to conform my lifestyle to the standards set forth in the Bible." The one who holds to the first statement is under no obligation to give up his worldly attitudes.

The head covering is so foreign to modern society that many professing Christians will go to extra lengths to misinterpret this passage to nullify their feelings of obligation or conviction. Books about the head covering surged when cultural changes demanded a rationale to no longer require it.

Many Christians in churches today are not even aware that the head covering practice exists. Upon encountering the passage for the first time, some readers discover that the command is clear and straightforward. If God allows the command to stand out, the Christian must then make a decision. Many resist this passage because it requires sacrifice. They read more into it and study the passage, the history, and the cultural setting, all to prove it is unnecessary for today. Others read misleading text notes that explain the passage away. Still others, since they have never known anyone who practices this doctrine, including their spiritual authorities, assume they simply do not understand what seems so clear and so dismiss it. Yet a few will take the teaching to heart and seek to be obedient. God may even stir a woman to follow this Scripture before being exposed to it. Several Christian women have testified to a compulsion to cover their heads when praying, only to later discover this passage.

Rather than attempting to explain this or any other of God's commands away, our desire should be to understand His commands and please Him with our obedience. This chapter refutes common arguments against the covering. Even if this defense were completely thorough, leaving critics in silence, contention against this passage would remain, and for that matter remains against many passages in the Bible. Believers should not be easily swayed by seemingly authoritative arguments that undercut the "difficult" passages of Scripture, for it is written, "That we henceforth be no more children, tossed to and fro, and carried about with every wind of doctrine, by the sleight of men, and cunning craftiness, whereby they lie in wait to deceive" (Ephesians 4:14).

Argument 1: Doesn't it say in verse fifteen that long hair is a woman's covering?

This is a common question from those researching this Scripture. Yes, it indeed says in 1 Corinthians 11:15 that the hair is given to a woman *for a covering* (to be covered). But that does not nullify all that was previously written about the additional covering.

Verse six demonstrates that long hair is only part of the covering, and that the other part of it is a material covering. "For if the woman be not covered, let her also be shorn: but if it be a shame for a woman to be shorn or shaven, let her be covered." This verse would not make sense if hair were the only covering. How could a woman "also be shorn" when she does not cover if her long hair were her covering? The two statements in verses six and fifteen could not be coupled appropriately unless it is assumed that two coverings are intended: her long hair and the additional covering. The two then appropriately make up the covering that Paul speaks about, and the passage reads correctly without confusion.

A look at the Corinthian church's response to Paul's teaching demonstrates that they interpreted the passage to mean a material covering, and not only the hair. In chapter eight of *On the Veiling of Virgins*, Tertullian, an early church writer, said, "Likewise, the Corinthians themselves understood him in this manner. In fact, at this very day, the Corinthians do veil their virgins [and married women]. What the apostles taught, their disciples approve."

The Greek language in which Paul wrote leaves no room for ambiguity. The Greek word for "to be covered" which Paul uses to refer to the artificial covering in the first verses is *katakalupto*. But in verse fifteen where the woman's hair is referred to as a covering, Paul used the word *peribolaion*.

Based on a distinction between the two separate Greek words, the New Revised Standard Version clearly distinguishes between hair and veil in 1 Corinthians 11:5-6:

> But any woman who prays or prophesies with
> her head unveiled disgraces her head—it is one
> and the same thing as having her head shaved.
> For if a woman will not veil herself, then she
> should cut off her hair; but if it is disgraceful for
> a woman to have her hair cut off or to be shaved,
> she should wear a veil.

Other authors cited throughout this book offer extended re-
futations to this argument (often with analysis of the Greek
words), including Climenhaga (1938, pp. 88-92), Wooten (1997
pp. 29-46), and Henderson (2007, pp. 113-115).

*Argument 2: The command to cover the head was just a tradition
that does not need to be followed today.*

Dismissing this command with the idea that the instruction
was just for one period in history is faulty. The reasons for the
covering—access to Christ, order of headship, prayer, proph-
ecy, the effect it has on the angels, the call to be modest, and
the physical witness a covering has—are not time-sensitive
traditions that pass away in a few centuries. Rather, Western
society sank into immorality during the twentieth century, pla-
cing the head covering in a hostile culture. Paul made no direct
appeal to a specific situation, period, or culture with which the
Corinthians were struggling.

In churches today, the word *tradition* often carries negative
connotations. Church music and service styles, for example,
have fallen into two categories: traditional and contemporary.
Whereas traditional implies "old, boring, and out-of-date," contemporary implies "new, exciting, and with-the-times."

Jesus had another idea of tradition.

> Then came to Jesus scribes and Pharisees, which

> were of Jerusalem, saying, Why do thy disciples
> transgress the tradition of the elders? for they
> wash not their hands when they eat bread. But
> he answered and said unto them, Why do ye also
> transgress the commandment of God by your tra-
> dition? For God commanded, saying, Honour thy
> father and mother: and, He that curseth father or
> mother, let him die the death. But ye say, Whoso-
> ever shall say to his father or his mother, It is a
> gift, by whatsoever thou mightest be profited by
> me; and honour not his father or his mother, he
> shall be free. Thus have ye made the command-
> ment of God of none effect by your tradition. Ye
> hypocrites ..." (Matthew 15:1-7)

Jesus makes it clear that the commands of God are not traditions. Instead, traditions in this context are the ways people
attempt to justify and nullify the commands of God to fit their
culture. From this point of view, it is not those who are obedient to the command of wearing a covering that are "traditional,"
but rather those who attempt to invalidate the Word of God
through their own cultural "tradition" of not wearing a covering.

Even though wearing the covering is not a tradition as Jesus defined it, many translations render *ordinances* in 1 Corinthians 11:2 as *traditions*. Indeed, the word *tradition* in the
passage from Matthew is the same Greek word that the KJV
translates *ordinances*, so *tradition* in Matthew and *ordinances*
in 1 Corinthians is the same Greek word. Nevertheless, the
word in 1 Corinthians is presented in a different way from how
Jesus presented it, for this tradition was of God.

Even then, one cannot be sure that Paul was referring to
the covering as one of these good traditions. If he was, he was
also calling Communion a tradition, since he addresses both as

companion issues. In 1 Corinthians 11:2, Paul says, just before speaking about the covering, "Now I praise you, brethren, that ye remember me in all things, and keep the ordinances, as I delivered them to you," while in 11:17 he says, just before speaking about Communion, "Now in this that I declare unto you I praise you not, that ye come together not for the better, but for the worse."

Paul seemed to think that the church needed to improve the practices of wearing the covering and partaking in Communion, whether or not he considered them to be traditions. Either way, just as Communion is practiced, so should the covering be practiced. The commands stand as just that: commands to be obeyed and practiced with a willing zeal to good works (Titus 2:13-14).

Argument 3: The command Paul gave for the covering was just for the Corinthian church.

This statement runs into two problems within 1 Corinthians. One is in 11:16: "But if any man seem to be contentious, we have no [other][8] such custom, neither the churches of God," and the other is in 1:2: "Unto the church of God which is at Corinth, to them that are sanctified in Christ Jesus, called to be saints, with all that in every place call upon the name of Jesus Christ our Lord, both theirs and ours."

In both passages, Paul makes it clear that the principles in this book are not only for the Corinthian church, but for all churches that call upon the name of Christ. Since the name of Christ is still called upon by churches today, then the writing is for everyone at any period in time and at any place in the

---

[8] *Other* is added for contextual clarity. *Other* is used in translations such as the Amplified, NIV, and NASB.

universe that a church might be found, regardless of culture.

Even with these straightforward commands about to whom these passages apply, dissenters may argue that if Paul asked for uniformity among the churches, the common practice then today would be to not wear a covering. Again, this argument picks apart one verse in the passage, ignoring the eternal values and reasons for wearing a covering.

Against the argument that the covering was just a local Corinthian practice, Arthur Climenhaga, president of the Brethren in Christ Messiah College in the early 1960s, wrote in his thesis about the covering doctrine:

> A careful study of the epistle of 1 Corinthians in the earlier portion reveals that Paul denounced a party spirit. There were four parties at Corinth: Judaists, Apollos party, Paul party, and Christ party. If Paul denounces such a party spirit and tries to promote unity among the Brethren, why would he turn right around in the eleventh chapter and present a doctrine of the veiling only as a local issue—Greek custom for the men, Jewish for the women—and thus engender party strife worse than in the first case? The only answer is that the doctrine is not a local custom; it is something which is based on eternal foundations.

Tertullian also wrote about the universal application of the head covering in chapter two of *On the Veiling of Virgins:*

> Throughout Greece, and certain of its barbaric provinces, the majority of Churches keep their virgins covered. There are places, too, beneath this [African] sky, where this practice obtains; lest any ascribe the custom to Greek or barbarian Gentilehood. But I have proposed (as models)

those Churches which were founded by apostles
or apostolic men.

Paul clearly intended the instruction to apply to all Christian churches, and the early church writers clearly understood it
as such.

*Argument 4: Paul commanded the Corinthian women to cover their
heads so they would not be like the "shorn" women.*

This statement is a half-truth. The concept comes from certain translations of 1 Corinthians 11:5, among them being
neither the King James Version nor the New International
Version. The translation used here is the New American
Standard Bible: "But every woman who has her head uncovered while praying or prophesying disgraces her head, for
she is one and the same as the woman whose head is shaved."

The "woman whose head is shaved" refers to immoral women in Corinthian society. Some writers claim that Corinth
was a particularly wicked city, and prostitutes had certain customs of shaving their heads; thus a special command was
needed for the women in Corinth. However, there is no reason
to believe Corinth was any less virtuous than other coastal cit-
ies in the region. By having long hair and covering their heads,
the church women were adhering to another principle, stated
in 1 Thessalonians 5:22: "Abstain from all appearance of evil."
In the case of hair and head covering, Paul commanded the
Corinthian women to do just that. Nevertheless, this is not the
only reason women were to follow God's commands. Other
reasons are stated in the text other than in verse five.

However, having long hair and a covered head did indeed
separate the Corinthian church women from the pagan women,

perhaps more because of cultural decay than an effort to make the church women distinct. When a Christian walks out the principles in the Bible, his very way of living, being, and appearing will be remarkably different from the way the rest of the world exists, even in supposedly moral eras (Romans 12:2). Wearing a covering is not about being different from the rest of society for the sake of being different; it is about being obedient to Christ. Visible separation is usually the product of being obedient to Christ, and is thus valuable as a measure of discipleship.

Coincidently, women today can once again apply the argument of not being "like the shorn women." Now most women in Western culture cut their hair short and do not wear a covering. Women who are obedient to the covering doctrine appear just as different from the rest of society as they did in Corinth years ago. This difference in appearance is nothing to be ashamed of, but rather something for which to be thankful.

In conclusion, even if there was a culturally sensitive contrast for the Corinthian women at that time, it does not nullify the universal reasons to wear a covering Paul clearly taught. The culturally sensitive contrast itself may well apply to our day, as well.

Argument 5: Paul was biased against women and was oppressing them with the command to cover. Since women have more freedom today, we should not follow this teaching.

Much of the way Paul addressed women was revolutionary for the time. In Romans 16:6, 12, 13, and 15, Paul sent greetings and blessings to many women who were working hard to bring honor to God's kingdom. He cared about women and treated them as fellow workers. In Philippians 4:2-3, he wrote,

> I beseech Euodias, and beseech Syntyche, that
> they be of the same mind in the Lord. And I in-
> treat thee also, true yokefellow, help those wo-
> men which laboured with me in the gospel, with
> Clement also, and with other my fellowlabourers,
> whose names are in the book of life.

He was not rebuking these women and telling them to stop working for the kingdom of God. Rather, he was telling them to agree so they could continue to work actively for God, as they had been doing with Paul for some time.

Regarding the doctrine of the covering, Paul reinforced a blessed principle not to oppress women, but to give them the freedom in Christ that he enjoyed. In 1 Corinthians 11:11-12 he cautioned men not to use their headship position to oppress women. He demonstrated that men and women are dependent on one another in the body of Christ. The covering, he wrote, is not representative of oppression, but is rather a symbol of authority, power, and glory.

Paul taught truth to help men and women recognize where God could use them best in the body of believers. He did not limit anyone's potential for God to use him or her to the very fullest. If all women acted like men, where would be the motherly figure Paul took special note of in Romans 16:13? If all men acted like women, who would be the head of the household and provide for the family? Part of God's curse to Adam and all men involved their masculine role and the difficulty of providing for the family through their work. For women it pertained to their feminine role and the pains of childbirth.

Argument 6: But my translation of the Bible says ...

Bible translations abound. Some translations dilute or nullify certain truths. What Paul wrote to Timothy proves true: "For the time will come when they will not endure sound doctrine; but after their own lusts shall they heap to themselves teachers, having itching ears" (2 Timothy 4:3).

The passage in 1 Corinthians 11:1-16 has perhaps suffered more than many other passages in the Bible. Take the New International Version, for example. While the translators did accurately portray the doctrine in the main body of the text, they included a footnote of commentary with another rendering. Capitulating to dubious translations held by certain groups, the NIV translators offered an alternative rendering of 1 Corinthians 11:4-6 in the footnote:

> Every man who prays or prophesies with long hair dishonors his head. And every woman who prays or prophesies with no covering of hair on her head dishonors her head—she is just like one of the "shorn women." If a woman has no covering, let her be for now with short hair, but since it is a disgrace for a woman to have her hair shorn or shaved, she should grow it again.

The Message, a paraphrase of the Bible, reckons 1 Corinthians 11:1-16 practically unrecognizable. Though the book's preface includes a disclaimer that it is not a translation but a paraphrase, it is often used by readers as a translation. Dubbing it a paraphrase does not justify inaccurate paraphrasing. Observe the verses from 1 Corinthians 11:1-16 from *The Message:*

1-2It pleases me that you continue to remember

and honor me by keeping up the traditions of the faith I taught you. All actual authority stems from Christ. [3]In a marriage relationship, there is authority from Christ to husband, and from husband to wife. The authority of Christ is the authority of God. [4]Any man who speaks with God or about God in a way that shows a lack of respect for the authority of Christ, dishonors Christ. [5]In the same way, a wife who speaks with God in a way that shows a lack of respect for the authority of her husband, dishonors her husband. [6]Worse, she dishonors herself—an ugly sight, like a woman with her head shaved. This is basically the origin of these customs we have of women wearing head coverings in worship, while men take their hats off. By these symbolic acts, [7-9]men and women, who far too often butt heads with each other, submit their "heads" to the Head: God. [10] Don't, by the way, read too much into the differences here between men and women. [11]Neither man nor woman can go it alone or claim priority. Man was created first, as a beautiful shining reflection of God—that is true. But the head on a woman's body clearly outshines in beauty the head of her "head," her husband. [12]The first woman came from man, true—but ever since then, every man comes from a woman! And since virtually everything comes from God anyway, let's quit going through these "who's first" routines. [13-15]Don't you agree there is something naturally powerful in the symbolism—a woman, her beautiful hair reminiscent of angels, praying in adoration; a man, his head bared in reverence, praying in submission? [16]I hope you're not going to be argumentative about this. All God's churches see it this way; I don't want you standing out as an exception.

This paraphrase compromises God's commands to suit man's worship style. No matter how many false teachers and doctrines people heap before themselves, they as mere humans do not have the power to change the truth God has given man in the written Word. These people attempt to justify themselves in such matters to their own destruction instead of willingly submitting to the teachings of God, who sent His Son to the cross so that all men might be given the opportunity to turn away from their sin and accept the will of the Father as their final authority.

Argument 7: I want to cover my head, but my husband does not approve.

A woman who wishes to wear a covering for the first time may be instructed by her husband not to do so. The wife must either continue wearing the covering in disobedience to her husband or not wear the covering out of submission (Ephesians 5:22). Both decisions appear as contradictions. The commands of God have precedent over the commands of man. However, this is no excuse for a wife to disregard her husband, which may do more harm than good. A wife must first be sure she is in subjection to her husband, "that, if any obey not the word, they also may without the word be won by the conversation of the wives; while they behold your chaste conversation coupled with fear" (1 Peter 3:1-2).

The woman may demonstrate to her husband why she desires to cover through her deeds, showing that her Christian devotion touches all areas of her life. She may work toward unifying the household and making it a place of love. Few women who grew up in veiling churches have the opportunity to face such a challenge in order to win the privilege to wear the head covering.

Even after all avenues are pursued, it may still take time

for her loved ones to accept the covering. The wife should be patient, go slowly, and set her husband at ease through her submission, not running ahead of him, so that he does not feel threatened by this change. Many husbands have been won over by a wife's patience and submission. With discernment, she may gently inquire if there would be times he would be comfortable with her wearing the covering, perhaps in private prayer or around the home.

A woman in such a difficult situation must be strong and trust God and not despair or lose patience. One solution may not suffice for all women facing this problem. Remember to seek the Lord's will first in obedience to the husband, obedience to the scriptural commands, and harmony among family members. God gives hope to His people when they are struggling.

In conclusion, section one identifies four reasons for women to wear a covering: to honor the headship order, for the sake of the angels, for modesty, and for a sign and testimony of devout Christianity. The covering is to be worn not only during times of prayer or while busy in other Christian duties, but as often as possible, in recognition of the four reasons in Chapter One to wear it. Because the covering is not practiced in Western society today, there is much resistance to this teaching. It is helpful to analyze common responses to the head covering so that we may encourage its willing and joyful adoption by Christian women.

Because conservative Anabaptist churches have historically practiced the covering doctrine, a host of new issues have been introduced. Since approximately the 1970s, new covering designs have threatened to replace the historic designs. The next section analyzes these changes.

Section II

Covering Style Changes in Conservative Anabaptist Churches

Introduction and Definitions

The following chapters will contrast the "veil" and other cloth styles (including hanging veils and doilies) with the "traditional covering" (pleated or gathered), or "cap." This section is intended primarily for use in Mennonite and Amish-Mennonite churches that are engaged in the decision-making process or that have recently adopted a cloth style and are experiencing unrest in their congregations.

Many devout Christian women wear veils. This is not intended to offend these people, but to show support for the traditional covering in our churches by discussing the deeper issues beneath the change. Indeed, the conflict of style change is not an isolated issue but is evidence that the church is struggling with the effects of broader changes in society.

While this issue may not appear directly connected to broader issues, the deep investment individuals have in the outcome demonstrates that no small issue is at stake. Further, the interest each party has in the outcome is much larger than is often acknowledged or realized. It is irresponsible not to consider the extensive ramifications in years to come from any seemingly small change. The decisions of today affect not only the Christians of today, but many generations and years into the future.

If a congregation or denomination lacks a God-rooted desire to uphold the practice of the covering, then a discussion about style is meaningless. If the spiritual life of an individual is faltering, if prayer is a meaningless cliché, if Bible reading is dry, then a discussion on style or on any other outworking of our faith is second in priority. If wearing any style of covering is rooted in compulsion, lifestyle, or a sense of duty to self, family, or culture, then it is not worn out of love for God, obedience to Jesus, or gratitude for salvation. When changes are made in style to make life easier or to be more socially acceptable, or when a style is retained merely for form or lifestyle, it does not matter which side of the argument one is on. An inner conviction is crucial (Matthew 23:23-28).

There are two primary categories of religious head coverings in use by Anabaptist women: traditional styles and cloth veil styles. For the sake of a clear definition, the traditional style is shaped like a cap or bonnet and consists of two pieces. The front piece, the brim, forms an arc around the top and sides of the head, coming up either onto the ears or just behind the ears. The back piece is either pleated or gathered to the brim. It covers the hair bun, allowing space between the material and the hair. In German, the *fedderdale* is the front part and the *hinnerdale* is the back part.

Most traditional-style coverings are made from stiff fabric, but some are made with pliable fabric. Some styles have a string sewed to each corner and tied together comfortably below the chin; others have longer strings that hang loosely down the front or back. Variations of this style are in use by the Amish (including Lancaster County), Old German Baptist Brethren, (Old) Mennonite churches and conferences, Beachy Amish-Mennonites, Holdeman Mennonites, and others.

Unlike the traditional style, the veil style consists of a single piece. It has no brim and is neither pleated nor gathered. This piece of loose fabric rests on the head and bun. A common cloth style is the hanging veil used by the Charity churches and some Beachy Amish-Mennonites and conservative Mennonites. Some veils are fastened below the bun, while others are left open. Extra material hangs below the bun to varying lengths, from just covering the bun to extending past the neck and down the woman's back. Cloth styles also include doilies and bandannas. A variety of cloths, colors, and textures are available, from transparent to opaque, from decorative lace-like designs to solid blacks, whites, and blues. The appendix includes photographs of various covering styles to further illustrate these definitions.

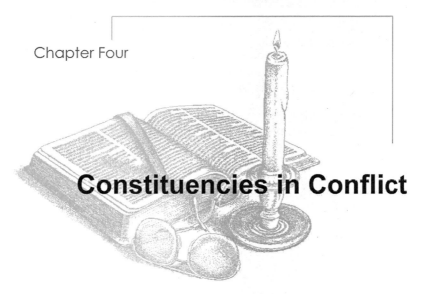

Chapter Four

Constituencies in Conflict

The desire to make allowance for a variety of covering styles, including the hanging veil and doily-like veils, has brought conflict to several major conservative Anabaptist constituencies, including the Beachy Amish-Mennonites and some Mennonite conferences. Little has surfaced in print that would give evidence of this conflict outside of denominational reports. This chapter provides an overview of past discussions and expressions about the covering style issue in order to present the current discussion in context.

Among the more succinct yet thorough reviews was Christian Hymnary editor John J. Overholt's article in the November-December 1993 issue of B.E.A.M. He wrote at a time when the hanging veil, once used only in Latin American missions, was first being adopted in the U.S.:

The writer believes that the new veil being adopted by some Beachy Amish-Mennonite churches is a step in the wrong direction. The Pan-American 1 Corinthians 11 opaque veil—kerchief-resembling, flowing veil, Central America model—which is making inroads, clearly does not meet the standard of the older historic veil, particularly in the following respects:

1) Recognizable and visible (not resembling the secular veiling)
2) Counter-cultural and identifiable (indicative of God and Christianity)
3) Distinctive and biblical (indicative of prayer and worship)
4) Having continuity and identity (indicative of ancient Anabaptist/Apostolic usage)
5) Having uniformity and witness (indicative of unity and power)
6) Having nonconformity and impact (not mistaken for harlot church veilings)
7) Denoting holiness and dynamic (not influenced by the flesh to world conformity)

Overholt included fifteen pictures to support the historical development of the "European veil." He wrote at a time when only several Amish-Mennonite churches had permitted the hanging veil.

Around that time, the first Beachy Bishop Committee composed a statement addressing numerous controversial issues, including the head covering. The document, *A Charge to Keep I Have,* gave several recommendations.

1) The covering should be religiously distinctive in appearance (a symbol of a religious application).

2) The covering should be large enough to cover (a symbol of obedience).

3) The covering worn within the church fellowship
should be of the same type (a symbol of unity).
4) The covering should be worn consistently
throughout the day (a symbol of faithfulness).
5) The covering should be of a solid color (a symbol
of simplicity and solemnity).

The document was never ratified. If it had been, the third
point may have ended the conflict within the denomination, as
few churches would have given one hundred percent support
for a change in style. In the years after, the Beachy churches
were increasingly unable to maintain a single style.

Only after another decade of appeals did the bishop committee, by then officially charged with "stay[ing] abreast of
trends or teachings that pose specific deceptive dangers to the
constituency," issue a statement and recommendation addressing the hanging veil by name. It was not formally adopted as
the sentiment of the constituency, but rather offered as a suggestion.

The bishop committee stated that several congregations
had requested assistance with the issue of covering style
change. The committee asked the questions: "Why the change?
What is the goal? Is the change to strengthen the application of
the headship principle, or is it for practical considerations
only?" The committee observed that some congregations had
completely changed to the hanging veil, while others had allowed both but each to be worn consistently. A few had requested that the traditional style be worn for church services. The
committee found that neither traditional coverings nor
hanging veils were made by most wearers, but were acquired
from others.

The committee recommended that a style change:

- Be preceded by "well thought through plans with prior set goals."
- Not become a "divisive issue—no church splitting!"
- Happen only after hearing the "wise words" of experience.
- Not be viewed as a way to regain covering size, as "those who choose to wear small coverings will probably do the same with the veil."
- Take into consideration that the "veil is not totally more convenient."
- Be of "white opaque material" and not of "varied colors."
- Reflect "both the sign and the symbol of the covering."
- Be free of "lacy or doily" ornamentation.

In conclusion, the document pointed out other groups that had lost the covering practice and that "any changes must be made on solid biblical principles" with a "need for messages and teachings on this practice" (Bishop Committee, 2002).

In 2004, the committee released another statement.

> One of the challenges is the way the veiling is worn outside of worship services. We are troubled by the growing number of variations in the practice for everyday usage that are not consistent with the way we expect its practice at worship services. We are deeply concerned that if we allow this inconsistency to continue unchecked, it will seriously erode both the principle and practice. We believe that proper biblical teaching and effective enforcement by us undershepherds are called for here and now to stem the tide and safeguard this practice. (Bishop Committee, 2004)

While concern was expressed with the variety of covering styles, the committee finished without specifying a pattern, allowing room for a variety of styles. Ministers may "prescribe the type and size of the veiling that is consistent with what we understand the Scriptures to teach."

However, consistency of covering style had been a concern prior. Sixteen years earlier, the "Observations" section of the Beachy Amish-Mennonite periodical *The Calvary Messenger* reported the following:

> A sister in another branch of the church was involved in a period of service in a prison ministry. She was asked to consider wearing a black veiling instead of her white covering. It was felt that a uniform expression would be less confusing to the prison population.
>
> This sister liked the veil and upon returning home got permission from her minister father to continue wearing it. Apparently, the uniformity principle was not the deciding factor this time.
>
> Bishop Harry A. Diener spent the greater part of his adult life at Yoder, Kansas, in the Mennonite Church. He has watched some developments of the last thirty years with a lot of disappointment. He told us that they began to lose the women's coverings when they lost uniformity of pattern. (Miller, 1988)

Since the late 1990s, a number of Beachy churches have formed constitution-based fellowships of like-minded churches. Among other expressions, the Ambassadors Amish-Mennonites, for one, included a constitutional statement giving clear direction for covering style. "The 'cap style' covering, with strings, is to be consistently worn and shall not be substituted with other patterns such as the black veiling, etc." (Article VII, Section 2b).

Like the Amish-Mennonites, Mennonite constituencies have also faced challenges in addressing covering styles. But unlike Amish-Mennonites, many Mennonites are arranged in conferences, where the larger body decides on practices instead of individual churches. If a single Amish-Mennonite church rarely makes a complete change of style among all women at once, then an entire conference of churches stands little chance of changing styles entirely. Thus, the tactic used at the constituency level is the same as is used at the church-level: get approval for two styles rather than a complete switch to veils. The case of the Southeastern Mennonite Conference is in this way similar to the Beachy case. It is different in that any change in practice must be agreed on by denominational leaders, rather than individual church leaders implementing personal visions apart from a decision at the constituency level.

Conference discussed the hanging veil in the late 1990s, and it was decided to continue using the prescribed traditional style. The written decision was supplemented with an illustration toward which sisters should be striving. In January 2006, a request once again came before the conference to allow the hanging veil. The request sparked many hours of discussion over the eighteen months following. According to the minutes, "Some of the concerns that brought this question were that apparently the hanging veil is used at home, for night traveling, and possibly even in public. We need to speak to the issue so that the hanging veil does not come in the back door" (SEMC, 2006).

In June, a resolution was offered to "continue with the cap-style veiling at this time" and accepted, with a promise to discuss it in a private session. The resolution further stated that many ministers sensed a need for "a certain degree of spiritual maturity and administrative fortitude" and a concern about "the direction this could take us, how it would affect our relations with other groups, and unity within our group" (SEMC,

2006).

Conference took up the issue in a private session. The majority of discussion focused on one question: "How can we more effectively administer the approved veiling in our conference?" Concern was expressed about maintaining adequate sizes. Suggested ways to address this were to prescribe a written minimum standard, to teach, and to personally admonish. In addressing a potential change in style, many felt a need to "do better at consistently practicing our present application before adopting a different one" (SEMC, 2006). Though there was talk that allowing two styles need not be divisive, a non-binding vote showed a nearly even split between allowing both styles or retaining the traditional covering as the only acceptable style.

The private session also demonstrated the ability for one group's decisions to affect another. Someone read from the South Atlantic Mennonite Conference's standard for the application of the hanging veil and suggested a similar wording for a Southeastern Mennonite Conference statement. Although the two conferences had divided for geographical reasons in 1995, the new South Atlantic Conference was known as being slightly more permissive in practice. The group's decision to allow the hanging veil was noticed by Southeastern members. Likewise, the Southeastern conference's resolution in June acknowledged how this would affect their relations with other groups.

In the January 2007 conference session, the discussion was similar to the earlier private session. Another non-binding vote of the ministry revealed eighteen for allowing the hanging veil and nineteen against it. In light of this, in March at an open session, the Executive Committee's recommendation "that the issue of the hanging veil be laid to rest for the present" (SEMC,

2007) was voted on and approved.

Someone asked if case-by-case situations could be appealed. The moderator said that appeals have always been allowed. Conference then entertained the question of whether or not they should define exceptions. The Executive Committee stated, "We felt it best to follow our past practice of generally not speaking to bedroom wear, or of beginning to speak to the many different questions about exceptional situations that could arise." At the June meeting, the appeals process was tested.

> One of our district councils received a letter from a couple appealing for the wife to have the privilege of wearing the hanging veil. There are no special circumstances involved in this appeal other than personal conviction and practicality. In light of Conference's recent decision, we decided not to grant the request. (SEMC, 2007)

Thus, after a year and a half of discussion, the conference laid the issue aside for the time being. Yet, with a divided leadership, it may only be a matter of time before the issue is brought up again.

Chapter Five

The Symbolic Meaning of
Covering Styles

The actual text of 1 Corinthians 11 is silent on describing any specific elements of head covering design. Thus, we must determine a design that carries the essence of the Word of God in our present age. In pondering the constitution of a head covering, I identified two basic elements: size and symbolism. Regarding size, the head covering must actually cover the head to such an extent that it lives up to its name. Paul speaks of the literal act of covering the head (verses 4-5), even though he does not specify a size. Yet, if the covered head was the only measure of a "head covering," then *any* material could be used for this purpose: a large paper bag from your local grocery store could serve as a head covering—after all, the head *is* covered, and quite sufficiently. Similarly, a feed sack, a bucket, a wig, an octopus or a thick coating of shampoo could serve to cover the head in obedience to 1 Corinthians 11.

The "covered head" is important, but so is something that symbolically represents a covering, that communicates to the observer that this practice is of sacred significance. The world is full of symbols, from company logos, road signs, and money to the cross, hand gestures, and even written languages. It is not symbolism or "form" that a society likes or dislikes, but what certain symbols and forms represent. A paper bag on one's head is symbolic: people may look at the wearer and think she is a little off the deep end. The viewer sees a representation and interprets the meaning.

The example of flags illustrates better how symbolism works.[9] What makes an American flag so important to some Americans? After all, it is just a piece of cloth. However, when this cloth is deliberately crafted into the distinctive pattern of an American flag, it is acknowledged as representing an exceptional concept and treated with special care. The federal government provides extensive guidelines for the proper treatment of this symbol in the Flag Code. It cannot touch the ground. It should not be left out in poor weather or overnight. If it becomes tattered, special guidelines govern its respectful disposal. It should not be used in a commercial way or placed on disposable merchandise. Passionate debates raged in the 1990s over the constitutionality of burning an American flag in protest. What's the big deal? It's just a piece of cloth. But it is the distinctiveness of the cloth that makes it special; it is the values and symbolism embedded in that cloth which we acknowledge when we see a flag. We humans like to represent our orientations and messages in symbols, whether flags, signs, or written languages.

Of the 193 countries recognized by the United Nations, none have a plain cloth void of design for their flag. Intentional

---

[9] By comparing flags to the woman's head covering, I am not suggesting their equality in all domains. However, the concept of symbolism is shared in both. This illustration—like all analogies—provides insights but has limitations as well.

flag designs are distinct, rich with meaning and stories, distinguishable from other designs so as to not confuse the message sent. The fifty stars on the American flag represent the fifty states, and the thirteen stripes represent the thirteen original colonies. The flag of the United Kingdom is a combination of the crosses of Saint George, Saint Andrew, and Saint Patrick, which begs questions about the country's history. The eagle devouring a snake on Mexico's flag contains strong religious connotations for Native Americans, and to Spanish-Mexicans it represents a moral triumph.

All clothing carries a symbolic meaning. The head gear worn in various professions testifies to this. Compare the hats worn by firemen, cowboys, chefs, police officers, and airplane pilots. Each design is distinct. It is not confused with the hats worn by others. It gives them authority to take actions associated with their professions: putting out fires, rounding up steers, preparing gourmet meals, enforcing the law, and flying a plane. The authority comes from the way people interpret the symbol. Without their hat and other profession-specific garb, onlookers may be reluctant to view them as authorities in their field. If you boarded a commercial airline and the pilot dressed like a cowboy, you may have some hesitation about joining him for this flight.

The woman's head covering is, of course, more than a symbol of professionalism or a country; it is a sacred symbol, but a type of symbol nevertheless. It communicates a meaning. A Christian's garb, including the head covering, has much potential to communicate devotion and experience for the Christian. The fashion world also recognizes that clothing is symbolic and uses the power of outward clothing to advance its purposes, even to profess sin. Miss Manners (Judith Martin) addressed the symbolism of clothing in a column titled "Getting at the Symbolism of Improper Attire."

> Everybody talks about comfort. And everyone talks about self-expression, especially slaves to fashion. What no one says in these arguments is that clothing is a social language that everyone reads, consciously or not. Any job counselor, costume designer, or defense lawyer will attest to that. Is this shallow? Well, it is undoubtedly on the surface. But sometimes that is all one can see, and even those with the opportunity to dig deeper still have to deal with the surface. Unlike beauty or other physical characteristics, *dress is presumed to be subject to some degree of choice. You may choose to be as close or as remote from the prevailing convention of the time and occasion as you like, but the distance will be read as reflecting your attitude* [emphasis added]. ... Such symbolism is powerful, and those who use it to lie should not be surprised or offended when others take these statements at face value. (*Chicago Tribune*, 11/2/08)

Without any religious intention, Miss Manners reminds us that the symbolism of our dress is powerful. Notice the italicized portion. The covering (and clothes in general) makes a statement about the church and the people in the church. The design of the covering, like the design of flags, communicates certain values and orientations. Ironically, those who deny this may be guided by the very values they do not acknowledge. Donald Fitzkee, a Brethren minister from Lancaster County, observed in his account of the Brethren congregations in southeast Pennsylvania in the early to mid 1900s:

> [Religious] moderns argue that external appearance is irrelevant to faith. After all, a pure

heart is what matters to God. What right does the church have to tell individuals what to wear? Yet many moderns willingly clothe themselves in the garb of corporate employers who require particular styles of suits and ties.

There are two separate but powerful statements in the traditional style and the veil style. Much like a country's flag or the hat specific to a profession, the traditional head covering is fashioned in a distinctive way. The design is intentional in appearance, and therefore, wearers and viewers alike recognize that it has a distinct meaning. The respected Amish researcher John Hostetler (1993, pg. 240) went so far as to call it "one of the most symbolic of all garments among the women." He explains further: "The specific way in which the caps are made, including the width of the *fedderdale* ("front part") and the *hinnerdale* ("back part"), and the width of the pleats and seams, is a sacred symbol of the community... These shared conventions are given sacred sanction and biblical justification." The design is essential in making the covering a *sacred symbol of the community*. No random method and material that simply covers the head will do.

To name all 193 flags and explain the meaning of the design would be impossible for most, but a viewer recognizes a flag when he sees one because of its elaborate design. Likewise, even if the casual observer does not realize all the symbolic meaning of the traditional covering at first glance, he acknowledges it is designed deliberately to communicate a religious concept. The traditional covering is unmistakably symbolic, and this is good. A head covering honoring 1 Corinthians 11 must be symbolically recognized as a head covering of religious significance.

Ideally, we would like the head covering to symbolically represent the God-ordained concepts discussed in Part I of this book: the headship order of God's creation, a message for the angels, modesty, and a general Christian testimony of trust. Is that the meaning we derive when we see a cap style covering? If in town and we see a woman wearing a type of cap, the first association we make is *not* headship, angels, modesty, or Christian testimony. What the conservative Anabaptist insider sees is a woman affiliated with a particular church, be it Lancaster Amish, Midwest types of Amish, Old Order Mennonite, Beachy Amish-Mennonite, conservative Mennonite, or another group, or even a specific type of any of these groups. Is this ideal? Should our head coverings associate us with our particular affiliation? Should not our head covering communicate a message of headship, the angels, modesty, and Christian testimony? Should not our head coverings associate us with "just Christian" and not a man-made denomination? Perhaps. But what design does that? Let us return to this question in a moment.

Prior to the 2011 revolution, Libya had a flag that was void of most design, merely a dark green rectangle. Libyans may have recognized their flag, but those outside Libya may have mistaken it for a generic green cloth of no significance. Like the former Libyan flag, cloth styles lack an appearance of deliberateness and careful design; the only design elements of a white hanging veil are the white tone, the circular shape (when laid flat), and the seam along the edge. And like the Libyan flag, the hanging veil wearer still intends to communicate values, but this communication is hindered by its non-distinct design. The cloth style may be a covering to the wearer, but it may be more easily mistaken by "foreigners." Indeed, the design elements are so few and malleable that one can transform the hanging veil so its intended use and meaning is entirely hidden. If it is attached to the end of a stick, it turns into a white surrender flag. The white veil can also be used to wipe down a dirty window, serving as a rag, or be used to blow your nose, serving as a pocket handkerchief. The lack of symbolic design—and therefore the weakness of communicated meaning —becomes evident when the hanging veil is recontextualized. Put a cap style covering on the end of a stick and it is a covering on a stick. Press it against a dirty window and it is a cap style covering against a window. Try to blow your nose into it —it is not a handkerchief. Put it in a cradle—it does not become a sheet. Because of the rich, intricate design, the cap style covering is one thing and one thing only: a religious, sacred head covering.

A young lady who grew up in a non-Anabaptist home was convicted to dress modestly and cover her head. Her parents resisted, but when she came of age and left home, she was free to join a Mennonite church several hours away and wear distinctive clothes that harmonized with her convictions. However, her parents were still self-conscious of her manner and appearance when she visited home. They preferred she wear no covering. She negotiated with them, and they agreed to allow her to wear a white missionary-style hanging veil instead of the distinctive Mennonite covering when visiting home. To her parents, a generic design of ambiguous meaning was preferred over one that identified her with a specific Christian body that collectively practices a Christian doctrine. Many people passing her in public did not associate her with a distinctive plain group, even though she wore a cape dress. They knew what plain people dressed like, as there were

Amish in the area, but she was different enough with her non-descript hanging veil that they did not associate her with them. People stopped and asked her questions. Are you a nurse? Are you a Benedictine nun? Are you an old-fashioned waitress? Despite all other identity markers being intact, the hanging veil dissociated her from plain Anabaptists.

The woman who wears a cloth style veil may, through handling, further demonstrate its weak symbolic meaning. She may be less inclined to treat the veil with the care she would a traditional covering. It can join a heap of laundry. It can be pressed into a suitcase. Countries want their flags to be distinctive and recognizable; therefore, a flag's design is deliberate. When its design distinctively represents ideas, then it must be treated with greater respect. Most owners of a traditional covering do not toss it into a pile of dirty clothes, nor do they press it into a suitcase when traveling. It is treated with special care because the covering represents a sacred concept, a sort of symbol of Christian citizenship.

Now, if we (as conservative Anabaptist insiders) see a woman who is wearing one of our familiar white hanging veils or one of our familiar doilies, how do we interpret her head covering? I suspect most would not read her as "just Christian" or read into her covering the concepts of headship, angels, modesty, and Christian testimony anymore than most would read these into a cap style covering. Instead, most would identify her as belonging to some sort of conservative Anabaptist group, but unlike the cap style, that specific group association is unclear. Let us return to the above questions left unanswered. Should not our head coverings associate us with "just Christian" and the concepts discussed in Part I? If so, what head covering design does that? I do not believe there is such a thing.

Paul spoke of head covering especially in the context of the church setting. In the passages around 1 Corinthians 11, he speaks of communion and the parts of the body of Christ. It is fitting that our coverings associate us with our church; Paul appeals to this association in both the first and last verses of the covering passage. Our church groups embrace the afore-mentioned values of the head covering. If someone can read our affiliation, they can read our beliefs, more or less, by the group with which we have chosen to join.[10] To be readily associated with a specific church and that church's values is more a root Anabaptist concept than to be associated with "just Christian" and not an actual body of believers.

Like the detailed flags of the U.S. and Great Britain, the intricate design of the traditional covering tells a story that appeals to church predecessors and to a rich symbolism described in 1 Corinthians 11. It ties us back to generations of faithful Anabaptists before, all the way back to the martyrs of the 1500s and 1600s. They wore a distinctive cap style covering; though it has evolved some, the basic shape is still there.[11] To break with this symbol means that there has been a funda-

---

[10] The sheer number of our groups need not be viewed as merely a product of contentious factions. Rather, we can read it redemptively as varying streams of Christians who in different times and places came to similar conclusions, and that each desired to associate with an intimate network rather than aggregate all into an over-sized plain Anabaptist ecumenicalism. Having symbols that represent our group and thus our group's values need not preclude a different set of distinct symbols identifying another group with the same values.

[11] I recognize, too, that several conservative Anabaptist groups include cloth designs in their total head covering configuration. The Hutterites wear a cloth, but the Hutterite groups with the closest link to past practice also wear a cap beneath the cloth; more permissive groups have begun omitting this cap. Old Colony Mennonites similarly have a religious cap beneath their scarf. Even then, the outward Hutterite cloth and Old Colony Mennonite scarf have distinctive design elements that far exceed a white hanging veil and lack the fashionable elements found in doilies. They are also worn more as outer head wear than as a covering of religious significance (reserved for the cap).

mental change in our values as a people and our understanding of the covering. When South Africans voted to change their flag design in 1994, many especially wanted to remove the small British flag on the corner. The change of flag design symbolized many South Africans' resentment for British rule and a break from British influence. By removing the small British flag on their flag, they demonstrated that the British no longer had power over them. They changed their flag because the ideas it represented had changed.

The traditional style carries an historic precedent. The conservative Anabaptists have built an identity over many years and generations that has meaning to much of modern society. Its perseverance over many generations gives it stability, validity, and roots. This movement is not merely the product of the modern age or one generation's ideas. A distinct, uniform style is an appeal of legitimacy to others that this is a church practice and not a strange practice the wearer does on her own. It specifically identifies the wearer with an established, recognized Christian denomination that provides accountability and input into the believer's life. A style that does not readily associate the wearer with a church group suggests greater individualism and autonomy apart from whatever group that person belongs to (if any). Perhaps it may not be the intention of any individual to change the spiritual meanings by discarding the traditional style, but the symbolic meaning is burrowed into the group conscience. To strip the covering of the distinctive design is to call its final religious meaning into question. Strong associations with Scriptural concepts are made weak associations by disassociating oneself from a group that has long practiced Scriptural concepts.

To reiterate and summarize the case so far, the detailed

designs of caps identify the wearer with a specific Christian group. When in public we encounter a certain covering style, we do not directly think about the concepts of headship, but rather think, "That person belongs to a Beachy / Mid-Atlantic Mennonite / Eastern PA Mennonite / Amish / Holdeman / German Baptist / etc. group because that is a Beachy / Mid-Atlantic / etc. cap style. Being identified with a distinct Christian group identifies the wearer with the values that group stands for, including headship, which the covering is intended to symbolize." Thus, being associated with a specific group reinforces the spiritual beliefs behind the covering because we recognize the covering, recognize the group, then subsequently recognize all that this group stands for.

When we see a cloth style covering, the wearer could identify with any number of groups. By not associating the wearer with a group that supports the 1 Corinthians 11 teaching, the connection between the head covering as a symbol and the Biblical meaning is diluted. The person wearing a veil could belong to one of many different groups, even groups that vary significantly from Anabaptist Christianity. Indeed, most of the conservative Anabaptist churches that have adopted the veils are also disestablishing their association with our heritage in other ways. Cloth style coverings are the result of a church that has a growing cache of individualism and it further reinforces that individualism.

In addition to disassociating members from a plain Anabaptist church with a long heritage, the white hanging veil also opens the way much wider for members to adopt unbiblical symbols and meaning of fashion and individualism, making the sacred covering profane. Consider this illustration. The cap style covering design is like a painter's canvas that has been filled with a picture. When that canvas is given to another, they keep it just as it is. They see the painting and understand what they see. There is no room left on the canvas to paint the recipient's own painting or add personalized touches, unless in a very, very minor way. The picture on the canvas represents the details already added into cap style coverings: the pleats (number, spacing, width, etc.), the brim (length, shape, angles, curves, etc.), the material, and additional stitch lines, ruffles, covering strings, and on and on. Everyone in a church has the same painting with no room to add much of any personalized, individualized touches. The cap represents the peace and unity of the church, a major theme throughout 1 Corinthians. The common painting also stabilizes the church's values and ability to communicate these values.

What would happen if everyone in church were given a blank canvas, or one with just a few dabs? When you give people a blank canvas, they are going to use it to paint their own picture. There is nothing on the canvas, after all. It is calling for individualized expression. The large white veil has minimal design elements in it. It has no angles, lines, pleats, etc. The only design elements are the material and a turned-in edge. This covering is basically a blank canvas. The first generation adopting the big white veils may all embrace the blankness of the canvas as their sign of unity, but it takes little time for members to start adding personal touches to the blank canvas. Thus, what begins as a single canvas design (blank) eventually goes in a variety of directions, representing individualized choice rather than the unified testimony of the church. Individual choice becomes the symbolic message, not the association with a church that holds the values of 1 Corinthians 11 (and a constellation of other values).

Therefore, the veil opens itself vulnerably to guidance from the same design concepts as contemporary fashion. It is more susceptible than the traditional cap to faddish designs, such as a tight, form-fitting appearance or decorative fringes. Is this just the author's personal opinion? I was curious about the impression left on someone who studies and works with fashion and I showed a fashion designer (not a professing Christian) pictures of our various coverings. She was the one who suggested the veils tended to represent individualized style elements, while the cap style identified the wearer with a group choice in design elements. She was also the one who noted that the veils tended towards elements of mainstream fashion. As she studied the white and black veils, she noted elements of lace, decorative fringes, and a type of transparency that elicited a completely different response than that of the netted caps. She felt the design elements of veils borrowed largely from contemporary fashion in women's two-piece undergarments. The resemblance highlights the sexuality of the wearer. This was a shocking suggestion, that our sacred headdress could become symbolic of undergarments and promiscuity. I would encourage the reader to browse the photo appendix to assess her conclusion for yourself.

Individual fashion elements come to dominate the blank canvas of veils in such frightening ways as these. A church may start with a large white veil, but almost inevitably shifts over time towards cloth styles with as many design elements in number as the cap style, but of a very different nature and meaning. This brings attention to the individual and is of the same spirit as the plaiting of hair and the wearing of jewelry during Roman times (1 Peter 3:3).[12] It is but one of many small steps away from an appearance that speaks to others of Christian values through Anabaptist identity. Though a cloth in itself will not completely nullify a Christian witness, if other small steps are taken simultaneously, they amount to a giant leap.

Many women in conservative churches now wear name-brand sweaters, pullovers with logos or insignias, and light jackets off the department store racks, some of which are designed to be form-fitting. When worn with a generic veil style, this cloaking of the cape dress further disguises a non-conformed witness to society. As many other small changes are made—changes that are of themselves seemingly insignificant (pleats, elastic bands, belts, hair parts, sleeve lengths, dress form, etc.)—it dabs the entire canvas of our set-apart-to-Christ grooming and garments with small splotches so that after a while one cannot see any design identifying the individual with a body of believers. It removes one stick at a time from the beaver dam until the structure's strength against the current is sufficiently compromised.

After several additional small steps, the hanging veil, even a large white one, may be easily viewed by secular society as a non-religious head accessory. It may be confused with a kerchief worn to keep the hair clean in dusty wind or to keep the hair up when working outside. Such change in appearance may not be a complete abandonment of devout Christian identity, but it is enough of a generational change to promote further as-

---

[12] Hairstyles also draw attention to the individual. At one time, women puffed their hair. Then the fad changed to combing hair tight. Later, in parting the hair, they made all kinds of zigzag lines. Then, they pulled it down over the forehead, as was the fashion in society at the time. To show off the hair and draw people's attention to it is antagonistic to the very intent of the covering: to cover the hair.

similation in the next generation. The cap-style covering is not as easily confused with a non-religious covering. It is incompatible with fashionable garb and either-gender clothes because it so strongly associates the wearer with a group that believes contrary. It does not lend itself as easily to short-lived stylish alterations like lace or other ornamentations. It is a rebuke to the devil, a beacon to God's angels, and a spiritual helmet for the Christian warrior. "Symbolism" is not just a social concept —it is Christian.

There is danger in blurring symbols. Dissociation in dress, even among the well-meaning, may soon bring dissociation from other doctrines of the Anabaptist faith, if not in the present generation, perhaps in the next, as dissociation continues with the offspring beyond where the parents feel comfortable. Will the children be content with the changes of parents when the parents were not content with the position of their parents? Must every generation put their personal stamp on the church? Ultimately, this risks complete loss of the church's identity with Christ. Those who have gone this path continue to have religion, but they deny the power thereof (2 Timothy 3:5). Anabaptist convert Stephen Scott in his 1997 book *Why Do They Dress That Way?* foresaw this trend ending in one of two ways: "A form of clothing may result that is either completely fashionable or that is quite unique but no longer expresses the principle it was originally intended to." The desire to not be associated with conservative plain denominations has not only given rise to the veil as an alternative style, but it has brought entire denominations to question the practice itself. The churches that teeter between requiring and not requiring coverings are largely using abbreviated cloth styles. If there are attitudes in the church opposed to the statement the church is seeking to make and each pursues a personalized style, those attitudes may reflect how distant a person is from the Lord.

Outward non-conformed garb within the Anabaptist tradition is a blessing God has given to the denomination, and the volume of good it speaks to secular society is not to be disregarded, even if we fall short of the message that simple garb conveys. That it has built such a solid reputation of devotion, able to resist even some of our contradictions, is not to be taken lightly. It has proven a steady beacon. The traditional-style covering is part of the garb of this historic identity. What it and the rest of the historic identity need is to be harnessed by subsequent generations for good, to be filled with meaning and offered to true seekers in society as a working, living, devout expression of Christianity that has deep roots and a heritage of servitude to God. To plant new seeds (or develop a new identity) is a risk, for we know not what ground upon which the seeds shall fall. If we already have the tree fully grown, then let us bring forth fruits, for every year, for every generation.

But what does the cap style symbolize to those who desire the veil style? After all, people can read different meanings in a single symbol. If the cap meant all these Biblical attributes to everyone, then no one would switch. The remainder of this chapter will sort through the various meanings the cap and veil have for three types of veil promoters: those who want to disassociate with their local church and see the veil as symbolic of this disassociation, those who see the veil as symbolizing their group of friends, and those who pursue the values of society and see the vague design of the veil as more compatible with society's symbols.

First, some insiders may resent the cap, as well as other distinguishing garb. This resentment may have arisen from disappointments with the church or family. Those who grew up in a conservative setting and have been hurt by inconsistencies may wish to distance themselves from a conservative Anabaptist identity, either by blurring the distinctive practices in their lives or by discarding the symbols completely. The focus is on what must go; they do not know what they are moving toward for a replacement identity, but whatever is new and available at the time is usually acceptable. They have lost the vision to manifest Biblical values outwardly and symbolically.

Even society has noticed inconsistencies among conservative Anabaptists. Special attention has been given to the Amish in recent years, but other denominations are not excluded. Society reasonably expects a group that retains such a distinctive identity to be devoted to their cause—in this case, Christianity—but when they see inconsistencies such as family abuse or unrestrained youth, they make much out of it (and often *really* have to go digging to find something). Some are curious and write books, conduct documentaries, or produce television programs. Others chide and poke fun at the contradictions. Still others are disappointed that a group that could be held in such high esteem for their devotion turns out to be as carnal as everyone else.

There are certainly many reasons to want to dissociate from the inconsistencies. But will we achieve a higher standard of consistency by distancing ourselves from this historic identity? Will we achieve a higher standard by stripping away symbols that communicate deep commitment? Do we really resolve our inconsistencies by neutralizing the good instead of curing the bad? By and large, conservative Anabaptists are still held in high regard by society. It may be more difficult for those who grew up with this pattern to understand the message the traditional style covering and other distinct styles of dress and lifestyle send, but they hold a place of reverence and respect. Others may be a select group of non-Anabaptist seekers who wish to preserve their autonomy and not associate with the church they are at. Perhaps the double meaning behind the cloth style is that the wearer does not wish to be associated with a group, but "just Christianity." However, Paul—in 1 Corinthians 1:12-13—rebukes members for a factious spirit and taking on names like Paul and Apollos, as well as *just the name of Christ*. Names of subgroups are not the concern, but rather the contentious fracturing of the church. While wanting to be identified with Christ is a noble goal, the symbolic interpretation is that by not identifying with a church (and purportedly just Christ), the individual identifies more closely to individualism, just something she is doing on her own and for any number of potential reasons, all of which have less merit since she may be the only one doing this.

The 2006 Nickel Mines shooting swept up global attention and a sympathetic tone rarely seen in the press. It demonstrated the public's high respect for the Amish, despite the contradictions made public through efforts such as the *Amish in the City* reality TV show. The public sees something in the Amish (and other plain groups) that they don't have: a group identity and a purpose that transcends the fleeting pleasures and fads of the world. They think, society's obsessions with fads, gadgets, fashion, and reputation building must just bounce off them, must not even register in their minds. They have their focus elsewhere if they are willing to dress like this, in a world where fashion is the beast of power. Thus, the solution is to address contradictions by addressing undesirable elements, not removing symbols that represent devotedness. We must put our energy where the problem is. If we desire to disassociate symbolically with our church group, should we not also follow through and disassociate with the church altogether, terminating our membership?

But what of those who are satisfied with Anabaptism, those who are not changing styles because of discontentment? These are the second group. They see their decision to switch as motivated by the right reasons. They admire their Anabaptist heritage and identity. Indeed, there is much blessing to be found in such contentment. In regards to covering style, they have faced a different situation than those who desire to distance themselves from historic Anabaptist symbols. Changes occur around them nonetheless. Content though they may be, each must respond to the fact that people they know have adopted the veils, people they admire: kin, friends, co-workers, and other intimate, meaningful relations. Though content with their practice, they still desire to win the approval of others and make friends. They still desire to conform to what their family and friends are doing.

People like to become like the people they like. We know that "birds of a feather flock together," but we become ever more like the flock. A school of fish, for example, are able to alter their pigments—if ever so slightly—to look more like those they are around. We, too, have a tendency to subtly adopt the behaviors of those whom we admire in order to win their approval. We copy their speech and catch phrases, we find their ideas resonate with us, we become interested in similar hobbies, and we wear similar style clothes. If those whom we admire adopt a veil style, do we not desire to identify with them in this area too? We may see some validity in their reasons. Largely, though, we are prone to agree with them because we like to like what they like. We do not want to be a dissenting voice in the group with which we associate.

There is nothing inherently wrong with wanting to identify with a group of friends. However, at what point does this desire become an unhealthy drive? When would the desire to identify with a clique be sufficient justification to alter the expression of a biblical practice or historic church practice, and when would it be inappropriate? This desire should be checked by the potential side effects of a change. For this set of people, the desire for the veil is a desire to show people you are associating with certain friends. It may be hard to see this because it is an implicit pursuit. Several examples follow.

Many well-meaning people are searching for a type of religiosity that is "early Christian." They often find the veil is a better expression of Christianity's purest era. What it is an expression of is more often a group of people who embrace this framework than a reality. The style is appropriately associated with this network, not a concrete era, and onlookers sooner associate the wearer with a fringe, unaffiliated, unidentified Anabaptist group that broke from an established group than "early Christian." Former missionaries may want the veil because it feels like that is part of who they are. The large white veil is called, after all, the "missionary veil." The intended identity is in the name. Friends of former missionaries like what their friends like, so they want the veils, too. As another illustration, those who like strongly pietistic expressions of worship with few standards like the veil because their friends also like strongly pietistic expressions of worship, and they have the veil. But it is a different kind of veil from the missionary veil. Or, sports players may like yet another type of veil, because their friends are all wearing that kind of veil at tournaments. Large, white, opaque veils can be just as much a marker of the in-group (and the out-group) among one clique as small, flowery doilies are among another.

In arguing for the veil, the case, "I want to be like my friends," will hold little water. So, it is not brought up. It doesn't figure in to the debates. A case is built on a rationale that sounds more noble and Biblically-based. But, what isn't said may be the real driving motive. Is it not dangerous to tinker with the manifestation of a core doctrine because we want to do what our friends are doing? Our Anabaptist group-mindedness can be harvested for tremendous good if the lead fish in the shoal or bird on the perch has the right color, but the power is equally disastrous when the group is guided by ungodly motives.

The third group desires a change for reasons beyond being like their friends. They see the veil as a chance to belong with society in general. They resist Anabaptist identity because of what it is: a by-design prohibition against their desire to conform to societal fashions. Christian Light Publications has produced a Home Economics course that gives instructions for sewing a traditional pleated-style covering and a hanging veil. The writers recognized a subtle tendency toward cloaking Christian distinctives and felt it beneficial to include this admonition: "The Christian woman should carefully examine her motives in wearing a flowing veiling—lest she attempt to avoid appearing different from others when she goes about in public" *(Home Economics II: Sewing a Headship Veiling, Light Unit 5).* Yet they may not be ready to abandon familiar friends, family, and ways of doing things. Therefore, from within, they advocate for styles of coverings and dress that lend themselves more to secular fashion. A generic (or lacy) cloth better fits fashionable clothing than an old fashioned looking cap. Since they do not want to leave their church, they work through the church to try to expand the boundaries in order to bring in what they feel they need to do to accept the insignias of society.

Like in the above cases, a variety of noble-sounding arguments may arise to cover ignoble motivations. "Isn't the Bible sufficient? Isn't it the only source of Truth?" they may ask. "Why all the detailed applications of plain dress not clearly spelled out in Scripture?" This rationale is a versatile shell that can be overlaid on a multitude of issues for an easy answer, but it hides more than it resolves. If accepted, it would allow members to abandon most distinctive garb. Appealing to a Bible-only approach sounds like a convincing argument. Ironically, though, they prove that the Bible is not sufficient for their standard of judgment. These rhetorical questions are themselves a framework by which to interpret the Bible. However, the Bible itself does not support this framework. It does not state that all applications must be directly spelled out in Scripture to be "scriptural" or true. If the argument states that the only truth is that which is in the Bible, but the Bible itself does not say this, then the rationale contains a contradiction. God expects us to discern His Word (John 1:1) not just from literal Bible texts, but from discernment granted by the Holy Spirit.

What does the Bible say about itself? That it is "profitable for doctrine, for reproof, for correction, for instruction in righteousness: that the man of God may be perfect, thoroughly furnished unto all good works" (2 Timothy 3:16-17). The final verses of Titus chapter two are similar. The "good works" that are not spelled out in the Bible are just as much a part of the greater Truth as examples of doctrine given in Scripture. For instance, 1 Timothy 2:9 instructs women to dress modestly, not with braided hair or jewelry or expensive clothing. Yet, these are not the only specific issues, but provide a springboard for further discernment that is just as much Truth as the examples given. The hallmark of Anabaptist Christianity is that it is not just a set of ideas, but a tangible manifestation of a Christian lifestyle that works in today's, yesterday's, and tomorrow's culture.

As those who resist a distinct Christian identity advance the argument of the Bible being the only source of truth, they find that the head covering, unlike other distinctive dress, is in the Bible. It remains that the head covering is a clear symbol that prevents them from total conformity to society. How do they get a rid of the head covering? It takes several steps. The strategy is to transform the doctrine into only an idea, not a symbolic practice. Doctrines are more easily lost when they are abstract concepts and not embedded in a strong symbol (i.e. tangibly lived out in our modern culture). Removing the symbolism of the covering is the intermediate step to eliminating the covering altogether. Symbolism is removed when the style is changed from something distinct—rich in shapes, lines, and contours—to something bland. Therefore, changing the style to something less distinct is a step towards weakening the doctrine. Caps speak more strongly of a religious motivation than veils, which are void of design.

When Scriptural associations are made weak through vague symbols, it gives contenders a greater foothold in challenging the whole legitimacy of the covering: "Is the covering a literal command, or are we just required to act out the principles without the literal symbol?" The first of such challenges may be a shock, but as more are emboldened to challenge the covering altogether, it is apparent that the symbolism has been drained from the covering over time. Thus, by changing styles and thereby changing symbolism, a group once devoted to the biblical practice of the covering may in time face challenges to the actual practice of the covering. No amount of deliberate strong teaching or emphasis on the practice itself can make up for the ground lost to the erosion of symbolism, neither can stipulations that say the veil is to be this way or that size or without such and such.

Switching to cloth styles is not the only approach to removing the covering. In the first half of the twentieth century, the steps described above happened in the Church of the Brethren in Eastern Pennsylvania. They also struggled to maintain the practice of nonconformity, especially in women's dress and coverings. It followed that those women who adopted stylish plain dress or secular fashions had to either shrink the cap significantly or secure allowance for wearing another style. At that time, flowery hats were the fashion in society. The women also desired to don "gay dresses [that] replaced modest cape dresses." Allowance of the hat would allow women to wear fashionable clothes, whereas the traditional style of the Brethren clashed with stylish garb. Some became so self-conscious of the covering that, for example, "a girl in the Lititz congregation. . . delayed joining the church because she feared her covering and bonnet would elicit ridicule from classmates" (Fitzkee, 1995).

Today, Mennonite and Amish women would feel extremely self-conscious wearing a flowery hat. Fashions change and reflect the values of that age. Whatever the next fashion is will make so much more sense because it reflects the values of the next age. The fashions of the past will seem so passé, anachronistic, and even downright ugly. Just as young people in the world today ridicule the fashions worn by their parents 30 years ago, so will what is considered fashionable today be ridiculed in the future. Peter Hoover, author of *Secret of the Strength,* made this observation in 1999: "We become detached from the world's things to the degree that we attach ourselves to Christ." A person's style of dress reflects his attitude toward the church, his fellow Christians, and his Lord. What does the covering say about our commitment to Christ? Obedience to Christ always comes with a price; therefore, Jesus urged us to count the cost.

In summary, the cap style head covering is a detailed design that is highly symbolic. The symbolism rests in its distinct and intricate design and its uniform and historically consistent practice by Anabaptists. It is therefore better able to communicate a meaning, most importantly the religious meaning discussed in 1 Corinthians 11. Symbolism is thus an essential Bible concept. When a distinct design is changed to a design that is vague, has no historic precedent, and has not been associated with a Christian-Anabaptist heritage, the doctrinal associations are made weak, if not intentionally, then in effect. Switching may also undermine the unified testimony of the church in its practice of this doctrine by accommodating those who want to disassociate with distinctive Christianity, those who view the veil as the symbol of a clique, and/or those who want to dress fashionably. By switching to cloth styles, a church is losing a small portion of the doctrine, no matter what the motivation of the individual.

Chapter Six

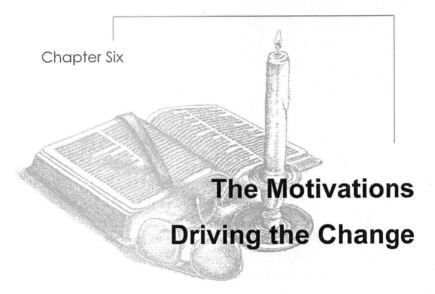

The Motivations
Driving the Change

Only recently have cloth styles such as the hanging veil become a popular alternative to the traditional covering. The idea to switch has spread from church to church with reasons given such as ease of construction, ease of cleaning, cost, comfort, opaqueness, and even more "Biblical." These are valid concerns, and it is not the pure goal of this book to dispute each in turn. However, are these the only reasons? Though practical reasons are often given for changing styles, are other motivations providing impetus for the change?

Humans tend to talk to others in the way they feel others will receive them best. For example, the child who requests his father's permission to visit his friend may be asked what he plans to do. He tells his father that they will be playing a game. This is true, but what he did not tell him was that they also plan to go for a bicycle ride along a busy road. If he told his father that, then he might not have permission. Therefore, he tells his father what good, safe activities he plans to do and leaves out the ones that may bring disapproval.

When confronting an issue, we humans naturally present information and arguments that make our case look good and try to clear from memory any information that would discredit our case. Are there reasons that go unstated when we consider covering style changes? As individuals, we at times are unaware of the root desires in our hearts for any issue. We tend to believe what we hear from others is true for us also, and we tend to hear that which is good, that which wins our approval. In one study, researchers measured the brain's response when the research subject viewed political campaign ads from a candidate they supported and a candidate they opposed. The researchers found that people tend to mentally block out the message of the opponent candidate, registering no emotional response—in essence, apathy. When they viewed ads by the candidate they supported, the study measured a strong positive emotional response. Given a choice, participants (and humans in general) will not choose to view information that challenges what they believe. In a well-cited study of change, the researcher found five steps in individuals' considerations when confronting a change. The fourth step is adopting the change. The fifth step is only consulting information that affirms the decision to accept the change; information that challenges the change is filtered out if at all possible.[13]

We are social creatures, not purely individualistic, so is it even possible to claim that we make our decisions independent of others' influence? The casual influence of others is powerful. Godly pressure to make a change is edifying and transforms us

---

[13] From Everett Rogers' Diffusion of Innovation, Fourth Edition (New York: Free Press, 2003).

into the image of Christ, but change which derives from social pressure is dangerous. Godly pressure is the full truth, that which comes out after a thorough searching of motives and desires. For the boy who wants to visit his friend, he knows his true desire for the bicycle ride in a dangerous place, and for him to be voluntarily upfront about it will bring his father's direction into his life. His will, trust, and inner desires are submitted to his father, and our deep desires should also be submitted to our heavenly Father.

In Why Do They Dress That Way? (1997), Anabaptist convert Stephen Scott wrote:

> Many church leaders are tolerant with young people and hope that their frivolity will disappear with age and maturity. Sometimes this happens; in many cases, however, the styles and trends begun by the youth carry through to their adult years and become a primary source of erosion of dress standards. When each successive generation feels it must put its unique mark on the traditional dress, and few are content to dress exactly like their "old fogey" parents, there is little chance of reversal. (pp. 40-41)

The "Observations" section of the Calvary Messenger described this attitude too:

> A non-local dad is reported to have complained that his daughter is expected to wear a covering like his wife wore ten years ago. Maybe this man should be thanked for putting into words what seems to be the attitude of far too many people. Such people are either incapable of seeing the long-term implications of such shallow thinking, or there is a deliberate strategy to move toward blending into the societal scenery around us.

> Inasmuch as society at large does not acknow-
> ledge the Lordship of Christ or the authority of
> the Word, such a course must be considered un-
> acceptable if biblical integrity is to be main-
> tained. (Miller, 1989)

Immigrant groups have much in common with conservative Anabaptists in that they are not assimilated into contemporary society. It has been observed that first-generation immigrants do not assimilate into society. Rather, it is the following generations that assimilate, having grown up in the new country. For example, the large Italian immigration wave of the early 1900s ended in the 1920s. By the 1950s and 1960s, about three generations from the first immigrants, the Italians were mostly assimilated. Today, Americans do not think of the Italians—or Poles or Hungarians or Russians—who descend from that era as separate ethnic groups. Likewise, within our Anabaptist churches, assimilation rarely occurs all in one generation, but happens through changes made in each subsequent generation that blur our identity. In this generational assimilation process, we have at stake not only our ethnicity and cultural heritage, but our distinct, devout expression of Christianity.

Scripture warns us that some changes come because ideas are introduced to us while we are unaware of the root or the consequence of the idea.

> Beware of false prophets, which come to you in
> sheep's clothing, but inwardly they are ravening
> wolves. (Matthew 7:15)

> And that because of false brethren unawares
> brought in, who came in privily to spy out our

liberty which we have in Christ Jesus, that they
might bring us into bondage. (Galatians 2:4)

For there are certain men crept in unawares,
who were before of old ordained to this condem-
nation, ungodly men, turning the grace of our
God into lasciviousness, and denying the only
Lord God, and our Lord Jesus Christ. (Jude 4)

These verses may seem harsh, but they highlight key words
and phrases: unawares, privily (secretly), and in sheep's clothing. In some churches, the switch to a cloth style has been one
of the first steps to losing the covering altogether. The attitudes expressed in the desires to change must be probed and
honestly discussed.

Could it be that the unmentioned reason why congregations
are changing to the hanging veil is that other individuals and
congregations are doing so? A group of like-minded churches
ought to look to one another for support and encouragement.
Such closeness brings Christian intimacy. It can also transmit
ideas quickly, whether edifying or not. The fads of the day or
pressure from other churches should not be steering the discussion as unspoken motives, but rather the issues of nonconformity, separation, meekness, love, and unity of witness. A devotion to these principles will likely be absent if the motive to
change is wrong.

Cloth styles are a new idea. In several communities, when
one church switched to the hanging veil, discussions took place
in neighboring churches about what this would mean for their
congregations. Churches whose members wanted to keep the
traditional style were under pressure from other congregations

to conform.[14] Is this a present-day fad or a lasting change toward greater godliness that will persevere through coming generations? How can we tell?

A good place to begin the probe is to ask this question (about covering style issues or any proposed change): "Why has this come to our attention and become an issue at this time?" Then follow it with another simple question: "Why has another topic, such as the wearing of feathery/flowery hats to church, not come to our attention and become an issue at this time?" While this question may seem ridiculous, the answer reveals much about why the first issue is an issue.

Such hats were the issue in transitional Anabaptist churches in the early 1900s (Fitzkee 1995). No person then would have thought of desiring a hanging veil. A veil did not resonate with that age. The sisters then did not see anyone who wore a veil. Flowery hats were what women were wearing then. Today, no woman would want to wear a flowery hat. The flowery hat is not in style. To wear one would send a confusing message to others in the church. They want something that is understood by their peers in this age. Fashion feeds off people's anxiety to do what other people do. Would a sister from the early 1900s prefer to wear a flowery hat or a hanging veil in our present age as an alternative to the traditional style?

Look at it the other way: would a church sister today who wants to wear a hanging veil want to wear one if she lived in the early 1900s when flowery hats were in style as the altern-

---

[14] For example, in central Virginia, where there is a cluster of three Beachy churches, the first permitted veils in 2008, the second in 2010, and the final in 2011. Similarly, in Plain City, OH, the three Beachy churches all permitted veils within several years leading up to 2008. The veil similarly spread through select churches in Northern Indiana and in Holmes County, OH. Interestingly, at the time of writing, none of the Lancaster County, PA, Beachy churches have permitted veils, though it has been discussed. Following this pattern, if one would allow, several others will soon follow.

ative to the traditional style? The reason the hanging veil is an issue today is because it carries a message of some sort that is pertinent to this era. We understand it to mean something about the woman who wears it.

If a church is considering an alternative style for the sake of convenience and practicality, it may justifiably ask why no exploration has been made into a variety of styles. Why only the hanging veil? Use the following as a test of sincere motives. Churches often pit a cap style against a large white veil, just two options. The veil at first seems more practical and "spiritual" than the cap: it is purportedly easy to make, is easy to clean, is not as see-through, and can flex when leaning against a pillow or whip-lash protector. The cap has a distinctive design—as discussed in the chapter on symbolism—that is precious to associating it with the values of our faith and in preserving it from faddish abuse. Why not introduce a third option: the covering worn by the River Brethen? (If you are not familiar with this design, it is listed in the covering style photo index under Brethren.) Just like the cap, it is easy to make, easy to clean, is not as see-through, and can flex leaning against something. In addition, it carries the distinctive design of the cap. Further, it is more practical than either the Mennonite cap or the cloths because it requires few additional accessories to keep it attached to the head. It fits snuggly but comfortably on the head; for extra security, covering strings may be tied under the neck. How practical!

"You're not seriously suggesting we switch to these coverings?" you may ask. No, I am not. But really, now, why do we oppose this alternative? With what look are these coverings associated that is objectionable? Is there a compelling reason they could not be seriously compared on the same basis of practicality as the hanging veil? A push for change that only includes one other option should alert church leaders and congregations to a limited goal, a single underlying desire. If we cannot accept the River Brethren covering with more enthusiasm than cloth styles, then something else is of more driving interest than "spirituality" and "practicality." Something is there that begs us to maintain our cap style covering, lest we change a sacred symbol for the sake of unaccounted motives covered up by noble-sounding reasoning.

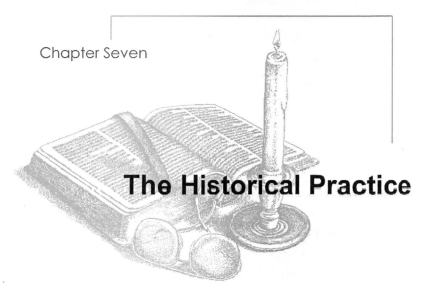

Chapter Seven

The Historical Practice

For approximately two millennia, Christians have intentionally applied the practice of the head covering. With that much precedent, Christians may analyze historical practices to gain insight for present-day direction. Three periods receive the most attention: the early church, the early Anabaptists, and "how we've always done it." There are underlying assumptions in any use of these three as justification for a certain style: the first two require the individual to believe these were periods of high spiritual fervor and insight, and that therefore the practices of the period are worth copying. The third offers respect to the precedent our parents set, as they respected their parents' Christian devotion. The only one of these three periods that can speak for itself is the final; the other two is always, in some way, a product of selected facts that the framer has chosen to advance above others. Such is how we write and frame history, and such framing should not go unconsidered in when the terms "early Christian" and "early Anabaptist" are dropped.

The early church sounds like the best period in which to seek a precedent, but the early church as a single entity did not exist. Churches in the first and second centuries stretched from India to Spain, from Ethiopia to the British Isles. In some places, the churches were persecuted severely, while in others Christians quickly gained a cultural influence and lived in peace. The churches varied in practices, doctrine, and even the books of the New Testament they used as their canon. When one suggests that the hanging veil is a more biblical style, he usually means the style worn by the early church. After all, the early Christians must know best what the apostles meant when they taught churches to observe this doctrine.

With all the diversity in the many early churches, the chances of them all having a common covering style are slim. Yet, a fabled "early church covering" exists in our minds because of how history has been selectively framed. This early church covering is imagined to be something like a Middle Eastern Muslim religious veil today. However, this assumption is misleading: there were varieties of covering styles. Further, none of today's hanging veils match the etchings or busts of that era. Authors have mostly focused on coverings from southern Europe during the first centuries because, for whatever reason, that is where they have chosen to collect what little data we have on period coverings. Here I shall summarize some of their findings.

The Jewish veil was a long cloth completely covering the hair and falling down the woman's back and sides to the ankles. The Jewish veil did not cover the face; however, it could be pulled in front of the face if needed (McGrath, 1991).

This long veil was not a religious covering. The Jewish women used it for protection, as certain groups wear bonnets, scarves, or cloth veils over their regular coverings today. Underneath, Jewish women wore a coif, a "stiffened material head-cap," which Karen Johnson, who authored the book Headcoverings in the Twentieth Century in 1994, compares with the present-day style of the Old Colony Mennonites, who wear to church "a black lace cap with a tightly ruffled ridge extending from ear-to-ear across the top of the head, worn beneath a head shawl."

Secular Greek and Roman society did not require any covering in their forms of pagan worship (Climenhaga, 1938). For fashion, Greek women wore a pointed cap or a straw hat and Roman women wore a round cap (Johnson, 1994). Christian women likely wore their hair up in a bun, as would be in line with Greek and Roman customs of the time, evidenced by period sculptures.

Several authors analyze drawings in the catacombs of Christians in worship to build a case for a style. The Christians in Rome retreated to these underground halls of burial beneath the city during times of persecution. Thus, persecution was the context in which these drawings appear. The depictions of women suggest that they wore some sort of head covering, indicating that they took the biblical teaching literally. William McGrath (1991) found that etchings in the Catacomb of Domitila in Rome—dating as far back as A.D. 95—show "modestly dressed sisters wearing the cap type veiling." Warren Henderson, writing about the catacombs, also observed that women covered their heads, but emphasized the cloth styles. Tom Shank, writing a chapter in the Charity Ministries publication "... let her be veiled," felt that, from the catacomb pictures, there was no definitive style, but rather a variety of cap styles and cloth styles. Tertullian, in his discourse on the woman's covering in about A.D. 208, speaks of "linen coifs of small dimensions." He appealed to the women to wear larger coifs, or caps—again similar to the modern cap style, though they likely wore a weather-protective veil overtop.[15] He called for women to wear a covering large enough to cover the ears and not sliding back on the head.

Paul showed an interest in passing on traditions within God's framework. Arthur Climenhaga (1938) feels that Paul did not specifically prescribe a style and would have likely advanced the notion that local covering traditions be observed. He likely would not have advocated one style in places where other covering styles were already being practiced, as long as they served their intended purpose of covering and were associated with godly Christianity. Women in many cultures by nature's design already wore some sort of covering.

The hanging veil bears little resemblance to the long Jewish veil or the various styles worn by the early Roman church. The veils of a handful of Anabaptist groups claim influence from these etchings, but disparities exist between their final design and the etchings. The veils cannot be accurately thought of as a descendant of an imaginary religious-style early church veil. The only conclusion on style from the early church was that there was no intrinsically biblical style or design.

The "early church" was diverse not just in practices, but in theology. It was far from a unified movement; instead, lively debates ensued on basic theological issues. Such deviance in thought and practice is evident already in Paul's epistles, as he

---

[15] Tertullian also mentions "turbans and woolen bands," which were not similar to the Jewish veil, but were the fancy wear of the elite classes and didn't even cover the head.

attempted to correct fundamental errors. Such is an attribute of any young movement: there is much sorting to be had. Appealing to the early church to legitimate a certain biblical style is more an appeal to an elusive history to avoid confronting present-day concerns of head covering application. If anything, Paul's suggestion seems to be for us to consider the relevant issues in whatever time or culture we are in to implement a meaningful practice of this doctrine.

The Anabaptist faith and cultural tradition in which the head covering has developed extend back to the early 1500s. Unlike modern cloth styles, the cap style has a long history through generations of practice. During the Middle Ages, Catholic nuns adopted the long veil over the coif, but Christian factions such as the Waldenses in France and Italy used the traditional cap style (McGrath, 1991).

The Anabaptists maintained this style of covering. According to the drawings of Anabaptists in the 1685 Dutch *Martyrs Mirror*, the women's coverings were a continuation of the traditional cap style (see etching details below). The issue then was not as pronounced, as all women wore some type of covering. But Anabaptist women wore a plain covering. In the Netherlands, where Menno Simons lived, each province had a distinctive costume that was worn on formal and fancy occasions. Today these coverings are confined to costumes worn at ethnic festivals. If you would take one of these fancy bonnets and remove the lace and the various wing-style rims, you would have left the rudiments of the cap-style covering.

The everyday coverings of all women were functional and plain, but the women of high society wore a fancier covering when in public. Anabaptist women would not wear the fancier coverings. This did not brand them as Anabaptist women necessarily, because poor people also did not wear the fancier coverings.

Details of etchings from the 1685 Dutch edition of Martyrs Mirror. Left to right: Maria and Ursula van Beckum (Book 2, Page 65); Anneken Jans (Book 2, Page 143); Six Brothers and Two Sisters (Book 2, Page 83).

When the Anabaptists migrated to America, they found that their coverings and garb differed from their neighbors who had come from other parts of Europe. This melting pot spelled the end of distinctiveness for most ethnic groups, but the plain Anabaptists found their garb functional, modest, and humble, as well as a distinguishing mark of their church group. Their 300 year practice of this distinctive garb has resulted in its rich meaning, imbued over time with the churches' values. As each generation continues the practices of the previous generation, the symbolism of our beliefs remains stable and rooted. Symbols take time to develop.

Because Western society no longer practices the head covering, many Anabaptist groups have become content that wearing any covering is enough, even if it is fashionable. The devout Christians reviewed in this section avoided fashionable coverings when these were the alternative to a Christian covering. Whether the alternative to a Christian covering is a fashionable covering or no covering, Christian coverings ought not cater to either society's fashions or fads within the church.

In summary, the hanging veil is not a recovery of early church practice, as the widely imagined "early church covering" does not exist given the extensive diversity in the early church itself. The hanging veil is, rather, a sudden, dramatic shift in design and pattern away from the historic cap style with marginal, if any, influence from a narrow set of drawings from two millenniums ago. We need not look back to some distant point to recover an imagined authentic style when the cap style covering today has a several hundred year history to which we are presently connected. Through this history of faithfulness, our cap coverings have come to be deeply meaningful and richly symbolic, quickly associating our people with our churches and our churches' Christian values. In a fast-paced society where everything is changing to be purportedly better, the stability of longstanding symbols of Christian devotion is desperately needed. Adopting the veil will not generate a 2,000 year heritage, but simply represent a new thing people are doing today with a citation to the past. The style of the covering may seem trivial, but a church's decision to change the covering style may someday mean the difference between standing for the Lord through future generations and melding into the worldly church.

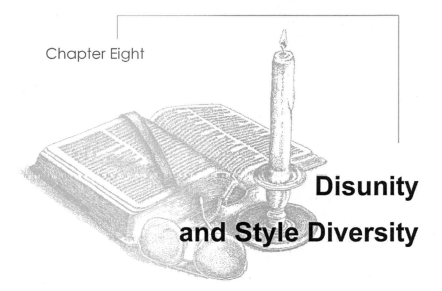

Chapter Eight

Disunity
and Style Diversity

The plain churches have a long history. They have had their proud moments and their ignominious moments. Plain churches that are faithful to the Scriptures still ask their people to submit to the authority of the church and avoid individualistic self-expression. Individualism stands against the church community because it stands against Christ. In Christ, we are to submit to one another, even when we are inconvenienced.

Although no covering design is specified in Scripture, the Apostle Paul called for a certain amount of uniformity in practice. The Corinthian church was known for its factions. One purpose of Paul's letter to the church was to encourage loving, sacrificial uniformity. This is seen in 1 Corinthians 1:10.

> Now I beseech you, brethren, by the name of our
> Lord Jesus Christ, that ye all speak the same
> thing, and that there be no divisions among you;
> but that ye be perfectly joined together in the
> same mind and in the same judgment.

At the end of the letter, he makes a direct statement that
the things he wrote were the commandments of Christ.

> If any man think himself to be a prophet, or spir-
> itual, let him acknowledge that the things that I
> write unto you are the commandments of the
> Lord. (1 Corinthians 14:37)

It is in this book that the ordinance of the head covering is
found. In defense of the ordinance, Paul wrote,

> Now if anyone is disposed to be argumentative
> and contentious about this, we hold to and recog-
> nize no other custom [in worship] than this, nor
> do the churches of God generally. (1 Corinthians
> 11:16, AMP)

Paul listed the head covering as an ordinance in conjunc-
tion with Communion. Just as he detailed the proper conduct
of the Communion service, he laid out the facts about the covering. The following instructions are given to new believers in
the Mennonite Church.

> By reading the verses carefully, we find the pur-
> pose of the ordinance. ... It shows the proper rela-
> tionship between woman, man, Christ, and
> God. ... The covering is a sign of power or author-
> ity which shows that the woman is taking her
> rightful place in God's order. ... She has both

power and authority in her prayer and Christian
testimony. Since the covering is a sign, it stands
for a pure devoted Christian life. ... Since this is
an ordinance of the Church, the Church should
decide the form of the covering since the Scriptures give no exact form. (Horst, 1934)

Thus, the Church has acknowledged its responsibility in
creating a unified and recognizable expression of the head covering for members. The introduction of cloth styles has allowed
for many contrasting styles that invite and encourage cliquishness. Often, to appease both sides of the issue, both the traditional covering and at least one cloth style are allowed to exist
side by side. This dual practice only shows the fracture in the
church, not its loving submission. The style of covering is then
no longer chosen by the church but by groups within the
church. The groups may coexist, but there is tension and judgment among the cliques. Such problems are not the exclusive
cause of cliques, but to allow the head covering to symbolize
cliquishness and personal opinions is to profane a sacred doctrine.

When the elderly wear caps, the middle-aged wear white
hanging veils, and the young adults wear small lacy cloths and
doilies, is there unity? When the ex-missionaries wear large
white veils, the converts wear opaque caps, the lifetime members wear traditional caps, and the sophisticated wear lacy
cloths, is there unity? When on Sunday mornings she wears
the traditional covering, on Sunday afternoons she wears the
casual black doily, and on Sunday evenings she wears the
dressy hanging veil, is there consistency?

One may respond that, as Christians, we should respect individual conscience and be able to tolerate differences and still

have fellowship. At first it may appear that each woman does what she pleases without interfering in the others' affairs and that all enjoy fellowship. But in time, as the more "modern" or "fashionable" gain the majority, the views of those who choose to retain the "old-fashioned" style are often discounted, and their voice in church counsel is often dismissed as belonging to the old school and shut out of serious church decision-making matters. Or it might work the other way: If a young sister wants to wear the old style, she is thought of as proud, drawing attention to herself, or needing to be different. Perhaps secret hostility arises for her failure to adopt what the others have, and there is a desire to push her out of the church.

The church is not living by Christ's standards if a person seeking to live in Christ is offensive. It is just a matter of time before the divisions in the congregation will show up in other issues. Can such a diverse array of coverings persist to the third and fourth generations? As discussed previously, the traditional covering is saturated with symbolism; it has meaning, and it suggests a story to be told.

For the young girl, observing the instability and inconsistency of the head covering practice shakes her security. She becomes less and less certain of the significance of the symbolism. She does not know who she should grow up to be, what identity, what role is expected of her as an adult. She is faced with an array of identities she must choose among. One covering style identifies her with grandma, another with missionaries, another with sports and recreation, another with her older sister, another with her friends, and none of them identify her clearly with the church body in the unity of Christ. Instead, she is taught that church unity is condoning differences.

The strength of a single style is the clearness of identity

with the church. Multiple styles dilute this symbolism, and the coverings take on other meanings, perhaps even superseding Christian devotion. The girl whose family moves to a new community nearly every year as she grows up faces stress and anxiety from the frequent change. She struggles to fit in. Likewise, youth growing up in a culture of rapid change face the uncertainty and instability of not knowing where they belong, who they are, or who they are growing up to be. When those frequent changes are also symbols that are supposed to have religious meaning, youth struggle to make sense of what Christianity is and what it looks like. Even when a church has clear doctrinal teaching, the instability and inconsistency that come from changes in religious symbols—such as the covering—have a destabilizing effect. Disunity prevents youth from choosing to identify with a unified expression.

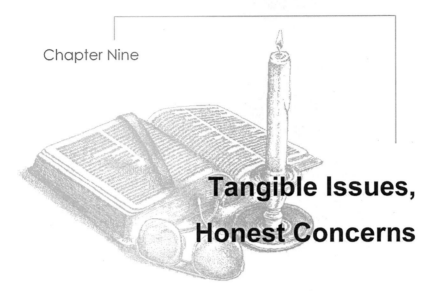

Chapter Nine

Tangible Issues, Honest Concerns

The intensity and length of the head covering style debate has produced a myriad of justifications for switching to an alternate style. Some are specific to the alternative in fashion at the time, while others have been repeated each generation, for flower hats in the early 1900s, kerchiefs at midcentury, or veils at the turn of the millennium. This section will address some of the more common cases.

Freedom of Movement and Practicality. In wearing the traditional covering style consistently, sisters may find that their freedom of movement is slightly more restricted than the women of society who goes without a covering. It is understandable that women may pursue some exceptions to consistently wearing a cap style covering. Some churches attempt to define the exceptions to the regulated covering style. Other churches prescribe the pleated-style cap for consistent and regular use with a few "goes-without-saying" exceptions, such as for nightwear. Many Amish, who may or may not have written Ordnungs, have historically permitted a kerchief or other cloth covering for domestic duties.

From the following excerpts of written standards, observe how various Amish-Mennonite churches either address the exceptions or allow unwritten discretion by not addressing the exceptions.

> Sisters' hair shall be neatly arranged under, and designed to accommodate, the approved tailored covering. Where an exceptional covering is required, only the church-approved white hanging veil shall be used.

> Sisters are to be faithful in wearing the headship covering, being careful not to substitute other styles of coverings or kinds of material for the type and style agreed upon by the church.

> Head coverings should be worn at all times for consistency of its design.

> The hair should ... be put up to conveniently accommodate a covering (white veilings are approved for nightwear and travel).

> Sisters and girls to be faithful in wearing their devotional head coverings. (Protective covering, such as bandannas and scarves, should not unnecessarily replace the devotional covering.)

Sisters are to be faithful in wearing the devotional covering at all times. It is to be of church-approved style and material to cover the woman's long hair.

The covering is to be of such a size and material to cover most of the hair, using church-approved patterns and material. If veils are worn, they are to be worn at home only.

Sisters shall be faithful in wearing the devotional covering. ... No scarves or veilings instead of the covering when in public.

The "regular covering" is to be worn when leaving the home. (The "cloth veiling" may be worn when visiting foreign missions.)

The traditional covering is to be worn for general use, with the exception being the opaque white veil fastened at the bottom, which is permitted for travel occasions.

Exceptions require a mature amount of discernment. Such allowances can turn into disrespect for the church when exceptional circumstances are sought and used to the fullest. The abuses are incremental. It starts by always being worn at home, then always worn outside doing yard work, then worn for quick runs up the road to neighbors, then a quick run to the store, then daily at the family business, then to informal church activities, and pretty soon, it is worn six days a week and the cap is just for Sundays. Women put on the veil when they get up in the morning six days a week, and put it back on by 1pm Sunday afternoon. It becomes a double standard. Pressure mounts to formalize on paper what already exists in practice.

A woman may be within the guidelines of the church, yet carry a spirit of dissatisfaction for having to wear the traditional covering. Children are watching their mothers, who set the precedent for consistency and support of the church when no one else is watching. A mother who tries to get all she can out of the exception conveys that attitude to her children in other areas. The father's attitude is contagious in the family as well; his indifference toward the covering is absorbed, and his indifference toward his headship role is felt.

The actual list of practical inconveniences circulating in our circles is long, far too numerous to weigh here point-by-point. This should alert our people to an abnormal obsession that gives far too much mental devotion to fault-finding. It is a powerful contrast to the spirit of contentment and yieldedness. Is the cap style really so intrinsically defective on every point? Or is it a spirit similar to the prosecuting lawyer, who in court must find every flaw with the other person, so that when the flaws all have been revealed, his point must be right by merit of the other being wrong? By only addressing the flaws of the cap, one may easily overlook the fact that cloth styles carry many of the same flaws, if not additional ones unique to its style.

Nevertheless, several of the more common issues will be weighed. One inconvenience is when the sister needs to rest her head, such as in a car, in an airplane, on a hospital bed, or in bed at home. When traveling, the headrest crunches the traditional covering if a sister lays her head back for a nap. In response, some churches have made allowance for the cloth styles on long trips. There are sisters who manage this allowance responsibly and there are sisters who take this allowance and spend the whole of their trip or vacation in a cloth style.

What they may miss is the opportunity to witness for the Lord about Christian faith and practice and to present a Gospel message from the authority of obedience to the church. Is there more interest in vacation pleasure than in witnessing for the Lord through distinct Christian garb in places where the message rarely goes? Whether we are comfortable with it or not, we are Christ's ambassadors, twenty-four hours a day, seven days a week, 365 days a year. We do not take time off for vacations, sabbaticals, or sickness.

As for other areas of impracticality or dissatisfaction with the traditional covering, most could be resolved by considering other historically grounded covering styles. Again, let us examine in more detail the possibility of considering styles such as the River Brethren, as one example (see appendix under Brethren styles). They wear coverings that maintain the identity and blessings of the traditional cap style and also have many of the practical features of the hanging veil. The material is opaque and is a soft fabric that allows room in the back without being formfitting around the bun. They cover most of the hair and come up to or onto the ears, and their design is naturally resistant to shrinking size.

In addition, the River Brethren covering is easy to slip on and off, making it quite practical. The traditional pleated-style covering is generally pinned to the hair. There are no fewer steps (and possibly more) in getting a hanging veil in place, also calling upon the assistance of pins and hair clips. Other soft covering styles that encompass both the identity and practicality issues are designed to be tied loosely under the chin or to fit snugly so that tying is not necessary.

Should we now expect our people to flock to the River Brethren style, which seems to incorporate the best of the traditional style and the veil? If the issue is truly practicality, with no underlying motivations, then could this alternative not be met with equal or greater enthusiasm than veil styles? Or, instead of wearing a hanging veil around the house, could a generic cloth be wrapped around the head, one that has the same practicality as the veil without the mold of a prevailing style? But a veil is generally the only acceptable option, for churches considering a change and for times of exceptions. Some motivation other than practicality is at work. What other people say, think, and do tends to influence us to a greater extent than any logic, sense, or book.

Is not practicality also one of the main excuses for modern fashion? Since the dethroning of the Victorian era in the 1920s, advertisements have emphasized the disposal of stuffy, difficult clothes in favor of whatever feels good and comfortable. While cost and comfort are certainly factors in selecting clothing, they should not be our primary motives. A focus on comfort and fashion leads to clothes that accommodate sensual activities. This is why in the 1920s activities such as casual dancing, sunbathing, and beachside beauty contests grew in popularity, while women simultaneously endorsed an end to the fuller, more modest dresses of the early century. A soap advertisement form this era demonstrates the spirit that modern fashion continues to promote today: "Youth demanded simple clothes instead of these fussy, elaborate styles of the 1900's. Clothes more expressive of youth's own slim, natural grace— clothes easier to wear in the thousand-and-one activities of modern women!" Personal pleasure was and still is justified by practicality.

Writing in response to the 1920s era of immorality, Daniel Kauffman stated in *Doctrines of the Bible* that Christians should have different motives for why they wear what they do: obedience to God, godliness, humility, purity, charity, self-sacrifice, temperance, modesty, joy of the Lord, reverence, integrity, and peace—all qualities that are at times in contrast with the spirit of convenience.

The covering is not always convenient. Yet, styles today are more practical than many of the cap variations of years gone by. An elderly sister tells the story of how her brand-new covering melted in the rain when she attended a youth activity. That's because the starched coverings of the time were ruined when exposed to the elements. Since then, the cap style has become quite practical in material and design while still retaining its basic character. Inconveniences ought to be worked with joyfully in light of Christian principles. If a woman allows the inconvenience to make her antagonistic toward the style of the covering, it may lead to a disdain for coverings in general. After all, true practicality is no covering at all.

The basis of our doctrine is neither practicality nor self-accommodation. All doctrine is based on obedience to the Lord Jesus Christ, the Head of the Church. Paul's ministry was not one of self-accommodation, but one of service and sacrifice to bring others to Christ, as He gave up what we value highly in our culture: regular meals, the opportunity to marry, and full financial support for his missions.

> Have we not power to eat and to drink? Have we not power to lead about a sister, a wife, as well as other apostles, and as the brethren of the Lord,

and Cephas? Or I only and Barnabas, have not
we power to forbear working? (1 Cor. 9:4-6)

What is my reward then? Verily that, when I
preach the gospel, I may make the gospel of
Christ without charge, that I abuse not my power
in the gospel. For though I be free from all men,
yet have I made myself servant unto all, that I
might gain the more. (1 Corinthians 9:18-19)

When ease and practicality are the weightiest matters with
covering style changes, the whole scriptural reason for the covering has taken a lesser place or has been lost altogether. Plain
people are sometimes asked, "Aren't you hot in those clothes?"
Our stand on modesty may have some inconveniences, but
there are also many blessings. A person was heard to say on
Good Friday, "I hope the heat has been turned up in the
church. I like to be comfortable when I remember Jesus' death
on the cross." The comment was said jokingly, but it is the
same attitude that is expressed when we require comfort and
convenience in serving the Lord.

The cap style is more convenient than it ever was in history, yet there is a push to pursue increasing practicality, almost as if practicality were an end in itself. While practicality
is certainly a consideration, and there are situations that de-
serve special attention in order to respect the covering and sus-
tain it as a blessing to the wearers, other factors, such as distinctive testimony, uniformity, and identity, are also worthy of
consideration.

The Size of the Covering. Every style of covering can be
made too small. The covering style has little to do with how

large the covering is. More important are personal conviction, influence of peers, submission, church unity, and church stability. In that a covering style change can come about through peer pressure and church instability, it is not surprising that the size of the covering does shrink at the time of a change.

The argument that the veil increases the area of covering on the head does not hold true for long, if it even begins that way. Members in many churches that have adopted cloth styles lament how small the veils have become. In the shuffle of changes accompanying style alterations, many sisters nibble down the size of the covering while switching styles. Is it common for congregations that allow new styles to actually have a fresh conviction for the covering, sparking an overall increase in size? If nothing else, the next generation learns that, first, the head covering practices are available for tinkering based of the fads of the time, and second, the change can be justified with spiritual-sounding lingo.

How much, then, should actually be covered? First Corinthians 11:15 lists the hair as one covering. Ideally, the hair as a covering indicates what area of the head should be covered —the area that brings forth the long hair. Yet many sisters, both those who wear the cap and those who wear the hanging veil, are content to cover the bun or the back of the head rather than the top part that produces the hair. This has been a problem for the existence of the church, as Tertullian, an early church leader, wrote:

> Others are to a certain extent covered over the region of the brain with linen coifs of small dimensions—I suppose for fear of pressing the head—and not reaching quite to the ears. If they are so weak in their hearing as not to be able to hear through a covering, I pity them. Let them

know that the whole head constitutes "the woman."

"It's not practical to cover the ears," someone may have said
to Tertullian. Evidently, Tertullian dealt with the same sorts of
perennial objections that float around today. His facetious
reply was far from accommodation. It has no parallel to the
suggestion that changing covering styles will solve the problem. He instead issues a rebuke and calls Christians to continue faithful practice.

The Transparency of the Covering. Opaqueness or
transparency is another issue often accompanying size. There
was a time when advocates of the hanging veil could argue suc-
cessfully that the veil was opaque and therefore concealed better than the cap. However, now that some congregations have
had cloth styles for a number of years—enough time to let it
evolve—the argument is visibly crumbling: veil material is becoming easier to see through. In addition, the veil material
clings to the bun and is tighter around the back of the head,
producing a sort of form-fitting headgear, whereas traditional
pleated coverings are designed to give the bun space and dis-
guise form.

Those who favor the veil have argued that if the netting
used to make the traditional pleated covering were used as
dress material, it would be unacceptable. This reasoning compares two unlike cases. Seeing the silhouette of a woman's bun
does not elicit the same reaction in men as would seeing the
silhouette of a woman's body. Furthermore, the objection does
not hold when applied to the veil. The material used for cloth
styles would also be immodest if used for dress material. Furthermore, the form-fitting clinginess of the cloth style would

accent feminine contours, something the stiff, cap style material would not do.

If a congregation has an honest, God-given conviction for opaqueness, the option remains to design a cap from opaque material while maintaining the advantages of the traditional design. Opaque traditional-style coverings are rare among the conservative Mennonites and Beachys, but closely related designs are used by various Old Order Amish groups in the Midwest, New Order Amish, and conservative Amish-Mennonite groups, such as the Berea Amish-Mennonites (see appendix). Indeed, to the traditional covering's discredit, some netting material has become far too thin and transparent and is of questionable value in covering the head. This in itself does not merit a switch to the hanging veil, but rather a renewed desire within a church or constituency to be covered and to use thicker material, like Tertullian's comments above.

Sewing the Covering. Another inconvenience is that many sisters are unable to sew the traditional covering; experienced church ladies have not passed on the knowledge and skill to the younger generation. Most sisters resort to buying ready-made coverings. It seems logical that if another style were easier to sew and cheaper, we should switch. And yet, if the sewing of distinctive cape dresses becomes too difficult, should we then stop sewing them? Will we do away with meals prepared at home because it is too hard and because fast food and prepackaged meals are readily available? The trend is towards consumerism—buying coverings, buying quick foods, and buying clothes rather than mastering crafts. To produce food and clothing for the family is to inoculate it against subtle value changes that come through dependence on the ready-made.

The making of the traditional pleated covering is a skill, an art that can be learned and appreciated. Christian Light Publications offers a Home Economics Light Unit with directions for sewing a traditional pleated covering. If more women knew how to make one, then would its acceptance increase? Learning to make a covering may instill a greater appreciation for the concept. With a little initiative, producing traditional coverings can be a restored art.

One woman from non-Anabaptist background pleaded with sisters in the church who knew how to sew the covering to teach her. Later she said, "As I sat and sewed each covering for my daughters, I would pray for them specifically. And as I saw the covering take shape, I was always humbled by what a privilege and responsibility it was to wear a covering. I thank God He has given me the grace to wear one, and I hope I am always worthy of what it means in my life."

Titus 2:3-5 reads in part: "The aged women likewise, that they be in behaviour as becometh holiness, ... teachers of good things; that they may teach the young women to be ... discreet, chaste, ... that the word of God be not blasphemed." The covering is part of being holy, discreet, and chaste. Therefore, the elderly sisters should pass on to the young sisters the skills for making the required covering for their church setting. Mothers should pass it on to daughters. Daughters should gain the skills to make coverings with the same zeal with which they learn to make their own dresses. The mother need not bear responsibility for passing on every skill to every daughter, but treat the family as a unit. Older daughters can teach the younger daughters so that all daughters can help their mother prepare meals and sew. The burden of all work need not rest on the mother.

To change the style of covering on the basis of an inability to make them is to admit that the church has failed in this area. If the skill necessary for making the required covering has not been passed on, is the teaching of why we wear the covering also weak or non-existent? It only stands to reason that changes in "nonessential" issues lead to moves in essential issues. We have time and energy to do what we want to do.

Changing styles with much caution. Leaders may approach style changes by calling for good teaching about the doctrine and making specifications about what is expected of members. This is supposed to counteract covering shrinkage over a transition period. Well meaning motivations are certainly evident. However, the fruits of this approach are limited if not also misleading. Good teaching does not prevent or recover that which is lost in the style change itself. It does not address the decline of strong symbolism that the cap style contained (as discussed in chapter six) nor does it deal with the fashion-conscious spirit appeased by the change. In addition, commitments to teaching are soon forgotten. Is it a good intention fallen short or a false confidence in our ability to control the situation?

What about codifying what is expected with standards and diagrams? When a change takes place, ministers may specify precisely what is expected in order to have a change in style without a loss of size or intake of fashion. However, the very need for more specific standards at the time of change is a testimony against the change. It demonstrates that, by changing the head covering style, the church is now more vulnerable to further erosion in practice. Where there is no threat to a given practice, there are few if any standards. Thus, in some way, switching styles makes the church more vulnerable. Even with the most detailed regulations, small signals of drift begin emerging within several months of the change in most churches, if only in what parents tolerate of their children and youth. What such seeds produce in 20 years can not only be left to the imagination, but demonstrated amongst the early adopters.

Maybe this generation of leaders and laity will guard the change very closely. Yet, the style change contains the seeds of its own undoing. Such a drastic, intentional change as altering covering styles starts a pattern of making more changes in future generations. Those standards designed to prevent further change are inadvertently conspicuous to the next generation. The standards become an easy, visible target at which to take aim. The regulations so carefully crafted now to accommodate cloth style coverings can be easily modified by the voice of a church or conference that has become accustomed to tinkering with standards. It is easier to modify the details of what is allowed with a certain style than it is to allow an entirely different style to start with. It is easier to allow smaller cloth coverings, to allow decorative fringes, and to allow flowery doilies along with hanging veils than it is to switch covering styles to start with.

Once the cloth style has been adopted, the largest hurdle has been overcome on the path to decorative small doilies, even if the initial adoption is fraught with regulations to prevent this end. Again, the seemingly cautious change to veils contains the seeds of its own undoing. When standards change now, they can change more easily later.

Cross-cultural and missionary situations. The hanging veil is often used on the mission field, presumably because converts can make the switch from no covering to a veil more easily than to a cap. In less-developed situations, the hanging veil material is easier to purchase than the netting, easier to keep clean, and easier to make. The hanging veil, it is argued, is more practical and culturally relevant. At one time and in some places, it may be. However, it has become an end in itself (the actual veil style) rather than a means to an end (a way to get natives to practice the head covering doctrine in a specific context). While veil materials were once readily available in host countries, now some missions are importing the tools and materials needed to sew a hanging veil. The reason for using the hanging veil in the first place has gone.

The veil as an end in itself impacts the home church. The missionary may continue wearing the hanging veil on visits back home and even on extended furloughs. Missionaries may face the temptation to define themselves by the veil, define themselves as different, rather than wanting to be like the brotherhood when with the brotherhood. Some missionaries, upon returning home after a term of service, may further be tempted to continue wearing the hanging veil whenever possible. Now the issues of cheap material, easy cleaning, and ease of construction are no longer confined to the foreign field. White hanging veils become a symbol for cliques of former missionaries. The missionary experience has defined the person, which can be good. However, when the former missionary does not allow ongoing experience with the home church to also define her, then it is damaging.

The home church may also argue that they are supporting those on the mission field by switching to the hanging veil. Are there not more substantive and meaningful changes the home congregation can make to support the activities of missionaries? The best change a home church can make is to nurture a zeal for church work. Missionaries face disillusionment with the church upon returning because it seems people are not as consumed with God's work as much. How much better to address this discrepancy between mission churches and home churches, than to pursue superficial changes like alterations in covering styles?

The hanging veil was first introduced through Latin American missions. Early Amish-Mennonite Aid workers in Belize used a mixture of hanging veils and caps, but the hanging veils came to dominate. The veil was designed by AMA workers for that time and place, with no intention of starting a revolution in covering styles. Yet, since those early church plants, the veil has spread to all Beachy-sponsored foreign missions regardless of culture. Even in the very countries of Europe from which the cap descended, the hanging veil is used. How, then, is the hanging veil culturally relevant when it is rubber-stamped in all cultures, countries, and economies? Are the arguments presented for its adoption on any foreign field the actual reasons its advocates favor the hanging veil, or are there ulterior motives? Is the veil an end in itself rather than a means to an end?

Instead of carrying what covering style we wish to wear to the mission field, churches should study the society in which they wish to live and learn what symbols are culturally and historically relevant there before proposing a particular style advocated by Anabaptist missionary culture or a mission agency. In some countries, the hanging veil associates Christian women more closely with groups like the Roman Catholics or Eastern Orthodox than does the cap style. In other countries, the hanging veil causes women to stand out just as much as would any traditional covering—thereby inviting criticism and persecution. In some places, converts ask why they have to wear a covering at all—especially if other Christian denominations preach against it. It is reasonable to base the decision of style in part on what materials are available for construction and cleaning. A covering style that works in one village will not necessarily work in another village or country.

One missionary in a Catholic country shared that the locals often asked the church women on the street if they were nuns. On the other hand, visitors from the U.S. wore the cap and were often asked if they were Amish. The international community increasingly knows about the Amish (and Anabaptists in general), and they expect us to be us. Is it not better to be identified with Anabaptists—which we are—than a religion we are not?

The Dunkard Brethren Church mission in Kenya adopted the hanging veil as a covering for natives, although the missionaries wear the cap style covering. This was accepted by the native Christians, but they were very specific about how the hanging veil would be designed because they wanted to make sure there would be no confusion between them and Roman Catholic women. The native Christians understood the united witness that a covering gives to a church. While the cap has at times been misinterpreted as a Catholic covering, it bears much less resemblance to the nun's veil than does the hanging veil.

In some third world countries, native converts to Catholicism or Orthodoxy may wear complex head garb, including a combination of decorated fringes, multiple layers, stiff pleats,

or special fabrics. Such elaborate head dress is far more difficult to construct than a traditional Anabaptist covering, but it
has not prevented these converts from adopting the practices of
the mother denomination. Some of the Mennonite Christian
Fellowship churches in Latin America, including the church in
Paraguay, have demonstrated that the traditional cap style is
practical, adaptable, and relevant in a mission environment.
The Eastern Pennsylvania Mennonite Conference has also suc-
cessfully managed the cap-style application in the tropical
countries of Paraguay, Guatemala, and the Bahamas. Many
other foreign Anabaptist missions have ably administered this
practice in a variety of climates and cultural settings.

Consider those natives who have adopted the veil as the
only option made available by the mission. At one such village
in Latin America, a native teacher decided to have "culture
day" at school, and she chose to dress up in New Order Amish
garb. After spending a day in a large opaque covering, she com-
mented, "I wish we could wear these instead of our old, hot
veils!" With one statement she made two points. Not only did
she identify a practical issue important to citizens of the trop-
ics—that cap fabric breaths more easily than the hanging veils
—but she demonstrated that our grass tends to appear greener
to those on the other side of the fence as well. Is it always better done a different way? Discontentment with what exists and
the craving to put a personal stamp on the way we do things is
a universal phenomenon.

In this era of religious tolerance, we must remember that
non-Christian religions like Islam and Hinduism require their
women to cover, and they usually require a cloth style. A covering style should be relevant in a culture, but not necessarily
what that culture or local religion already uses, as the covering

may lack distinctive meaning. In many situations, the traditional cap style is a suitable, practical method of applying 1 Corinthians 11 with which indigenous converts would gladly associate. People outside the U.S. and Canada are becoming increasingly aware of the Amish and Mennonites, largely through media coverage. We should use this to our advantage when traveling or living abroad.

Changing styles for converts' sake. Some ethnic church members argue that the hanging veil would make the Gospel easier to accept, because converts would not have to make such drastic changes in their dress to join the church. However, the most dedicated and sincere converts are often looking to identify with the church body. They want to join us, they like us, they want to be like us because they admire our Christian lifestyle. Most converts gratefully adopt the church's strong, stable symbols and heritage. Women feel privileged to wear a church's covering style that identifies them with their brotherhood and unashamedly lets the world—and friends and family—know where they stand.

This desire to be associated with the brotherhood is a passion for most non-ethnic converts to the Anabaptist setting, including this book's author and contributing writer, as well as our spouses, who have provided much useful feedback for this book. After giving up television, radio, secular music, secular entertainment, health insurance, life insurance, sometimes computers, sometimes social security and pensions, sometimes cars and electricity, the privilege of taking one's place among the brethren and being identified by the outside world as distinctly an Anabaptist or a plain person, specifically an Amish or a Mennonite Christian, is highly valued and much treasured, for the group of us and many of our convert friends. It is the new charter for our life. Most sisters coming in from the "outside" are honored to wear the covering and are humbled before the Lord God, that He whom they serve has led them into this obedience of His Word. One woman who attends a mainstream church has been covering with a generic cloth style, which itself is an admirable decision given the opposition women usually face when they do this. She shared this about her choice of style:

> ...It is rather unfortunate that some Anabaptist churches have gone away from the cap styles. Actually, I rather like cap styles much better than veils anyway because they look nicer, are distinctively Christian and Anabaptist! Obviously, I can't wear a cap even though all my doctrinal beliefs are 100% Anabaptist. I have no right to wear such a covering because of my church.

For converts, it is debasing, destabilizing, and confusing to have their experience used as a lever to change covering styles. When they have made the sacrifices and given up whole circles of family and friends to be a part of the church, an overemphasis on changing the details of dress is immensely discouraging. If a woman is converted from a world of sin to the plain expression of Christianity, then her gratitude for being saved from the vanity of life and the wrath of God makes the wearing of a covering a humbling experience.

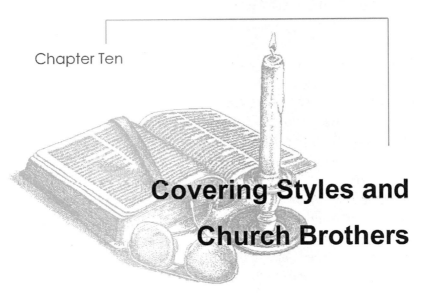

Chapter Ten

Covering Styles and Church Brothers

In many Mennonite and Amish-Mennonite churches, the level of outward nonconformity that plain churches require of men is disappointing. Since the introduction of factory-produced pants and shirts that are modest and cheap, brethren in the church have bought their clothes. Although there is not as much variation in men's fashion as women's, brethren can easily get caught up in what secular society says is classy, chic, and in style. There are fewer steps to take to cross the line, but they are subtle steps for men, depending on what is available at the store. When men dress to reflect their hearts' attachment to fashion, do they still strongly support a covering for the sisters, for their wives?

Would the men who advocate the switch to cloth styles be willing to do so if it required them or their wives to appear more nonconformed and separate from the world? Many men prefer cloth styles because they are less plain, bringing the women closer to the men's conforming styles of dress. Some men are embarrassed by how plain their wives, daughters, and church sisters look not only in public, but perhaps even more when mingling with fellow Anabaptists from other churches, such as at weddings or recreational events.

As leaders in our homes and in our churches, men should be leading the way in separation and nonconformity. At its core lies a saturated devotion to taking up our cross and following Christ, to interactive and inspiring times of prayer, to lively chunks of time studying the Word, with an all-around enthusiasm and contentment for all things involving the Spirit. We must crucify that in us which is of the world, not as an end in itself, but as a way to dislodge the distractions of this world which take our focus off God.

Men should endorse the Christian demonstration that the church we chose to join has held for generations, not as mere rules and standards, but as shared revelations of godly expression. We should be training our children and the brothers who look to us for spiritual inspiration in the way they should go, so that when they are old, they will not depart from it and can teach the next generation of church brothers. We should support our sisters, but not by agreeing with their complaints or campaigning for individual accommodation. (We would not expect our sisters to be silent when we become susceptible to such lusts in other ways.) We must stand for church unity and separation from the world. And if we require such from our church sisters, our wives, and our daughters, we must also demand it of ourselves.

Men often lead the way in an appearance that hides their distinct and outward separateness from the world unto Christ.

If the difference between men's clothes in society and in our churches is narrower than for our women, then men need to be very much on guard that they do not take the few small, subtle steps to cross that gap.

> In the 1890s Mennonite Noah Mack became convicted about his inconsistency. While traveling in their buggy, Lizzie, his wife, remarked as they passed another vehicle, "I guess they were Mennonites; she looked like it." Noah resolved that thereafter people would not know his church identity by his wife but by himself. (Scott, 1997)

Chapter Eleven

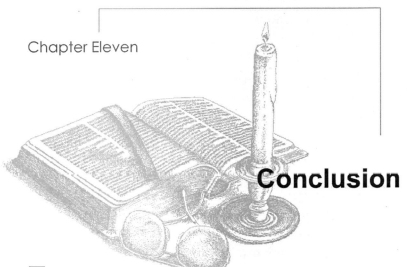

Conclusion

L et us reflect now on what has been presented. The woman's head covering is a sacred practice, a glorious yet tangible manifestation of the supernatural. It is a doctrine that embodies ideas about Creation, angels, the fashioning of man and woman, the order of the spiritual world, and even the supreme Headship of the Lord God Himself. So easily, the head covering can be profaned by using it for fashion and faddish change. So easily, do our humanly intentions defile these sacred ideas. So easily, such abuse is justified in the name of practicality, the "biblical" way, or another attractive argument. So easily, the covering is haphazardly modified, running after what others are doing, only to realize a generation or two later how silly such fashion looks, only to have spent our talents, time, mental energy, and spiritual stamina pursuing ballot measures, swaying public opinion person by person and chat by chat, and meticulously crafting plans of change designed to incapacitate the voices of concern. Yet, the next generation learns well and shows us how to do it better, breaking our hearts as they annul what we worked so hard to implement. What sort of overriding interest justifies this pattern, this obsession with getting what we want, this idolatry of the way we do things this generation? Is there power in the covered head when its doctrinal expression is tossed about like this? Let us reflect on this: the head covering is rightly reserved a place of sacredness, reverence, and respect, not an object of perpetual revision.

This book has attempted to practically apply Biblical wisdom for the protection of a sacred practice. Be this as it may, skeptics may conclude that there is actually no Bible-based rationale to suggest one style over another. It is with the cases presented in Section II in mind that we approach the verses that sandwich the Scriptural teaching of the head covering: 1 Corinthians 11:1-2 and 16.

> Be ye followers of me, even as I also am of Christ. Now I praise you, brethren, that ye remember me in all things, and keep the ordinances, as I delivered them to you... But if any man seem to be contentious, we have no such custom, neither the churches of God. (KJV)

> Pattern yourselves after me [follow my example], as I imitate and follow Christ (the Messiah). I appreciate and commend you because you always remember me in everything and keep firm possession of the traditions (the substance of my instructions), just as I have [verbally] passed them on to you...Now if anyone is disposed to be argumentative and contentious about this, we hold to and recognize no other custom [in worship] than this, nor do the churches of God generally. (Amplified)

Few other Bible teachings carry the appeals seen here. He emphasizes holding to the actual, literal practices that have been given them by verbal teaching and practical example, and seeks in 1 Corinthians 11 not to alter the practices themselves, but have the Corinthians understand the deeper meaning of what they are doing. He speaks of no specific design—indeed— but he speaks of revering that which is, that which is passed on verbally and by example from other Christians. God is pleased with their obedience to that which has been passed on to them orally. Customs, traditions, patterns: can such things actually be Biblical? Is obedience to such things to be praised?

Common customs provides a link to past spiritual teachers (those who have carried the faith to you) and a link to other churches. Our spiritual teachers today are, hopefully, the previous generation in church. Do we admire the gift of Christianity that they have preserved in their lifetime and given us? Do we admire it enough to want to possess an inheritance from them, to have a link with our forefathers? Or would we have been better off born into a jungle tribe of the Congo, a communist family in North Korea, an atheist mother in Western Europe, or a household in an inner city American ghetto? We may not have an ideal heritage, but we have an heritage that has permitted us to be devout Christians. The Corinthians did not stake their claim on Christianity by revising all the tangible practices they had been orally taught, all that they had learned by example of the disciples. Rather, to be connected into common customs and to live out that which was handed to you was part of the calling to Christianity.

Paul writes to them not trying to alter their practices—in as much as God is pleased with them—but to reinforce the deep meaning of what is being done. Where problems emerge

THE ORNAMENT OF A SPIRIT

in their practice of communion in the verses after 16, he suggests no sweeping revisions to the execution of communion itself, but an eradication of the sin that partakers bring to the table. When we feel there are revisions to be made, we do well to have a complete deference for that which has been handed to us, and a desire to enhance its features only with this sensitivity. For example, those who feel the cap material is not thick enough display more respect to the faith handed to them by keeping the shape and making it thicker than those who revise the entire form.

Is the influence of Christian predecessors or peers guiding covering style changes? Is a new covering style every generation—hats, kerchiefs, doilies, veils, and whatever may be invented next—in keeping with the spirit of the verses sandwiching this teaching? Does the covering connect you with a Christian lineage (which may have nevertheless fallen short in some areas) or does each generation set itself up as the supreme example in Christian devotion? Do we not see the same symptoms of such rapid, repeated shifts that Paul describes surrounding the communion table: factions among us (v18) and some running ahead of others (v21 and v33)? What all further direction was he going to give to the practices of the head covering and communion when he said, "And the rest will I set in order when I come" (v34)? The topics in this book—symbolism, motivations, constituency and church disunity, etc.—all seem to segue into the verses sandwiching the head covering teaching, hopefully giving it richer meaning. As Paul later came and verbally taught them further details worthy of the weight of written Scripture, may we also with gravity address very practical issues today.

Constituencies and churches that accept cloth styles rarely

reverse the decision. As long as the church chooses to uphold the cap style, the proposed change will continue to be brought up and evaluated; after the church changes, the issue is rarely revisited. Why not evaluate again and again and again after increments of time to see where it's going? Too many churches have allowed alternative styles only to end up with no covering one generation later. Many congregations and constituencies have decided against allowing the hanging veil, but the issue continues to be brought up by those displeased with the decision.

A sense of finality should be brought to the matter, and lingering complaints should be met with Christian charity and a desire to continue serving God. Often finality does not come until allowances are made. However, when a church steps back to re-evaluate the matter, especially as its fruit is witnessed, that church is seeking the fruits of a godly life and yielding self. God's will should be humbly sought and discerned in this matter, that He would reveal His wisdom to congregations and also reveal any false motives or inconsistencies that should be addressed. May God bless His churches with a deep desire to follow selflessly His commandments.

Bibliography

Ambassadors Amish-Mennonite, *Constitution and Bylaws of Ambassadors Amish-Mennonite Churches,* Article VII, Section 2b, 2008.

Beachy Bishop Committee (Ernest Hochstetler, presenter), *The Covering / Headship Veil,* 2002. Unpublished.

Beachy Bishop Committee (Bennie Byler, chairman), *A Charge to Keep I Have,* 1992. Unpublished.

Beachy Bishop Committee, *Presentation at 2004 Ministers Meeting by the Bishop Committee.* Unpublished.

Climenhaga, Arthur M., *The Doctrine of the Veiling,* Master's thesis, Taylor University, 1938. Available at the Menno Simons Historical Library at Eastern Mennonite University, Harrisonburg, Virginia.

Fitzkee, Donald R., *Moving Toward the Mainstream: 20th Century Change among the Brethren of Eastern Pennsylvania,* Good Books, Intercourse, Pennsylvania, 1995.

Henderson, Warren. *Glories Seen & Unseen: A Study of the Head Covering,* Warren Henderson, Colfax, Wisconsin, 2007.

Home Economics II: Sewing a Headship Veiling, Light Unit 5, Christian Light Publications, Harrisonburg, Virginia, 1993.

Hoover, Peter, *The Russians' Secret: What Christians Today Would Survive Persecution?* Shippensburg Christian Fellowship, Shippensburg, Pennsylvania, 1999.

Horst, John L., ed., *Introduction to Beginners in the Christian Life*, Herald Press, Scottsdale, Pennsylvania, 1934.

Johnson, Karen M., *Headcoverings and the 20ᵗʰ Century*, Karen M. Johnson, Modesto, California, 1994.

Kauffman, Daniel, ed., *Doctrines of the Bible*, Herald Press, Scottsdale, Pennsylvania, 1928.

Martin, Judith, "Getting at the Symbolism of Improper Attire." *Chicago Tribune*, November 2, 2005, sec. 8, p. 8.

McGrath, William, *Christian Woman's Veiling: A Biblical and Historical Review*, Amish-Mennonite Publications, Millersburg, Ohio, 1991.

Miller, David L., "Observations," *Calvary Messenger*, February 1988, p. 19.

———, "Observations," *Calvary Messenger*, November 1989, p. 20.

Overholt, John J., "Do Our 1 Co. 11 Veilings Have a Gospel 'Cutting Edge'?" *Biblical European Anabaptist Missions*, January 1994, p. 9.

Scott, Stephen, *Why Do They Dress That Way?*, Good Books, Intercourse, Pennsylvania, 1997.

Shank, Tom, ed., "... Let Her Be Veiled," Charity Christian Fellowship, Ephrata, Pennsylvania, 1992.

Tertullian, *On the Veiling of Virgins*, Translated by S. Thelwall.

Wooten, Mary, *When Women Go Under Cover: A Look at 1 Corinthians 11:2-16*. Master's Thesis, Grand Rapids Baptist Seminary, 1997.

Appendix 1:

Answers to Common Questions about Covering Styles

If you can see through the covering, is the head really covered?

The option is available to make cap style coverings opaque. A style change is not needed. To pose this question in support of a style change suggests ulterior motivations. The issue is material, not style.

Isn't the veil a more biblical style?

What is meant by "biblical"?

-I mean, that is what the early Christians did in Bible times.

Early Christians were a diverse group across a large geographic span and thus had a variety of styles, both cloths and caps. Even then, the veil alternatives today are nothing like the veils back then. Our modern veils have been invented in modern times.

-I mean, it is the style the Bible teaches

The Bible does not teach a style.

-I mean, the veil best fits the principles of covering the head.

Generally speaking, veils have no advantage over cap styles. If anything, by their detailed design, caps have more potential to communicate an idea, which are tied directly and indirectly to those very principles.

We can switch to a large veil and keep it from growing smaller through good teaching and being specific about what style we want.

Times change, and so do standards and practices. Commitments to frequent teaching are soon forgotten. Maybe you will keep it large, but what is to say the next generation won't? The veil pioneers in recent years started with very large, plain veils, intentionally; two decades later, they have lost ground on size and fashionable elements. This is because veils lack design elements and wearers soon fill the void with fashionable designs. The strongest, most durable practices are those passed from generation to generation.

Anyways, you lose the innate detail of the cap style when you switch to a veil, even a large veil. When you lose detail, you lose symbolism. This means you lose some of the connection between the physical covering and the doctrine. Could the call for more teaching at the time of a switch be a realization that we must compensate for the loss of religious symbolism?

A straight-forward understanding of the Bible and historical practice is a better basis on which to choose a

covering style than the current practice.

First, a straight-forward reading of the Bible reveals no concrete conclusion about covering styles. The fact that there is present debate over covering styles testifies to no straight-forward reading. Second, there was no universal historical practice for covering styles. The current practice of head coverings indeed seems to be in decline, but more so among those groups that tinker with style changes. Most Mennonite groups in the past few decades have first allowed cloth-style coverings prior to discarding the covering all together. Those groups most committed to retaining the cap style have also retained the covering. Finally, current practice is a very good measuring stick, because it is the world in which we presently live. The cloth styles are as much influenced by current practice as cap styles, and neither exists apart from the ideas of today.

We want to show support for missionaries by switching to the hanging veil.

For all of the things we can do to support missionaries, why this? When missionaries return home, they often struggle with members' lack of energy for church work. Churches can better support missionaries by having a zeal for church work comparable to mission churches. In light of this show of support, a change in covering styles is rather superficial.

It is the head being covered that is the symbol, not the physical covering itself.

Then anything could serve as a covering, whether a colander, milk crate, or paper bag. But the covering must be worn in reverence and communicate a spiritual concept. That means, not just any material will do. The physical covering itself must represent reverence and spiritual concepts. Thus, the actual covering is part of the symbol. However, the covered head is also symbolic. If the actual covering of the head did not matter, then it could be ever so small as long as it was still noticeable. Thus, the physical covering is a symbol, as is the covered head; they are inseparable.

The style of the covering is less important than the size.

1 Corinthians 11 does not discuss size and style. Therefore, we must identify a legitimate practice of this teaching for today. Neither size nor style nor color nor any other attribute is more important than the other in characterizing the covering. A five gallon steel bucket may be large and thus covers well, but we would have to conclude that it is stylistically inappropriate.

Converts from non-Anabaptist settings prefer the veil.

Many converts, if not the majority, prefer a covering style that unashamedly associates them with the plain churches. They do not want to hide this identity. Even those who do prefer veils are usually drawn to styles that would be too extreme for most ethnic Anabaptists. Converts should not be used to justify personal motivations.

We need to switch to the veil to make it easier for people to join our church.

The kinds of changes you make to win converts are the kinds of converts you will get. The changes you make reflect you more than imagined others. Dropping the covering altogether will make it easier for certain types of people to join our churches, yes, but what does this say about the depth of commitment of these converts?

I am not with a church that practices the head covering, but became convicted to practice it on my own. Are you saying I need to wear a Mennonite or Amish style covering?

No. God bless you for your obedience. Distinct styles are appropriate for those who affiliate with a group that practice the doctrine. For the woman who adopts the covering in isolation, a style that does not identify you with a specific group is expected. ...

If nothing else, switching to the veil is a good way to get a rid of covering strings.

Coverings and bonnets in the West have—with a few exceptions—come with strings, Anabaptist or otherwise. It is part of the covering. Some groups wear cloth style coverings with strings, too. Strings do serve a function, but past trends have eliminated it. Instead of having a single loop, cut the string in half, and tie it under your chin when you need some extra security to keep it on or in place, such as when it is windy. That is what it is there for.

For a church to regulate a covering style is unscriptural because it is adding to the Bible what the Bible does not say.

To insist on this point is just as much adding to the Bible because the Bible doesn't even make this point. The Bible does not say "no rules beyond Scripture" but says that it is profitable "...unto all good works" (2 Timothy 3:16-17), whatever they may be, explicit in Scripture or beyond. The "no rules beyond Scripture" argument is a versatile shell that can be overlaid on a multitude of issues for an easy answer, but it hides more than it resolves. If this claim is preceded by an explanation of what the Bible really means, then what has happened to the Bible text standing alone with no need to add to it?

We are switching for the right reasons.

Would not all people believe they have? The Bible teaches that motives can be subtle, especially wrong motives. Motives aside, this book has discussed basic, tangible advantages the cap style has which veils lack, advantages that enhance the identifiableness of 1 Corinthians 11 concepts. Motivations best align with realizations.

If the goal is to just preserve elements of a culture like the head covering, then it has no Biblical weight.

To divorce a culture from Christianity that has been so fundamentally influenced by Bible teachings over many generations is itself unbiblical. For example: "Now I praise you, brethren, that you remember me in all things, and keep the ordinances [or, traditions], as I delivered them to you" (1 Corinthians 11:2). Is not the hallmark of Anabaptism the implementation of Scripture in everyday life, so that all we do is inspired by Bible teaching? To study our culture is to study a very real attempt to make the Bible work in today's society. To separate the Bible and the culture is to reduce Christianity to ideas instead of practice.

I've read the book, but I just don't agree with everything.

Then maybe you agree more than you think. Part of the reason covering styles are changing is because of deeper motives, of which we may not be fully aware. If you're not sure why you don't agree, search for answers on that deeper level. The stated reasons to change may not be the real reasons, but distractions. Good, one-liner arguments sound nobler than revealing hidden desires. If there are subtle, deeper motives to change, then addressing the surface-level arguments will indeed be unsatisfactory.

THE ORNAMENT OF A SPIRIT

Appendix 2:

Caring for your cap
style covering

Coverings can quickly look drab if they are not properly maintained, and replacement costs can get out of hand. The dirt, dandruff, sweat, and oils of your hair and head can decrease the lifespan of a cap, but it does not have to. Like other clothing, caps need to be washed. Here is a quick and easy strategy to get the full life out of your cap style coverings.

Wash your covering at least once a week and as needed. Combine warm water and soap or vinegar in a plastic ice cream pail or similarly sized bucket and soak overnight. Alternate soap and vinegar each wash for best results. In the morning, hang your cap up or set on a towel to dry while getting ready. If you do not soak your covering overnight, a quick wash still goes a long way to extending covering life, or even a 15 minute soaking during the day. Occasionally do a touch-up ironing to reinforce features. For a crisp look, carefully use wax paper. Some wax will melt onto the covering and stiffen the fabric. Particularly stiff covering material does not need to be ironed.

In time, coverings do yellow. The best strategy is to cycle three coverings based on activity. Your newest covering is for church and formal occasions, your moderately used one for everyday use such as going out in public, and your oldest covering for gardening, lawn work, cleaning, and other dirty jobs. Continue to wash even the oldest covering to improve its lifespan, especially after a particularly dirty job.

Appendix 3:

Photo Index of Anabaptist Covering Styles

Old Order Amish constituencies have adopted a variety of two-piece caps to identify their group. They commonly have strings sewn to the lower front corner of the brim. The strings may be tied or untied and down the back or down the front. They may also be tied under the chin. The Lancaster Amish use somewhat flexible, somewhat opaque material. Whether the brim covers the ears or not varies by district and individual. The back piece is shaped like a heart. Occasionally, the Lancaster Amish may wear a cap made of black material. Most other mainline Amish, especially those in the Midwest, wear a large cap style covering made of opaque Swiss organdy material fused onto a sturdy fabric shell. This cap covers the ears, and the back part is pleated to the brim. Some more orthodox Amish groups, including the Swartzentruber, Nebraska, and Troyer Amish, use soft, cloth material in designing a cap, and pleat or gather the back part to the brim. These coverings are most commonly white or black.

The Amish-Mennonite cap style is worn by Beachy Amish-Mennonites and related Amish-Mennonite fellowships. The largest coverings are worn by conservative Amish-Mennonite congregations including Berea Amish-Mennonite, 'Old' Beachy churches, the Fellowship churches, and the Tampico Amish-Mennonites (also known as the 'sleeping preacher' churches). Some congregations use mesh material, while others have transitioned to opaque, lined coverings. These groups all wear the covering on the ears, and the brim covers most to all of the hair on top of the head. The smallest of the Amish-Mennonite style coverings are worn by mainstream Beachy congregations and cover the bun and a moderate amount of hair on the back of the head. Intermediate classes of cap styles are worn by some mainstream Beachy congregations, the Maranatha and Ambassadors Amish-Mennonites, and the Bethel Fellowship churches. (The Bethel churches have their origin in the Conservative Mennonite Conference, which used to be an Amish-Mennonite denomination.) Several congregations in these groups allow members to wear opaque, lined caps of intermediate size. These groups wear the cap anywhere from approximately an inch behind the ears to right against the back of the ears.

White and black veil styles consist of a single piece of cloth. It does not have a back piece affixed to a brim like the traditional cap style covering. The white cloth style ranges in size from the 'doily' to a long veil that drapes down the back, while the black cloth style is largely limited to small and moderate sizes. The adoption of veils has been mostly inconsistent among Anabaptist constituencies outside of the Charity churches. Unaffiliated congregations, especially recently established ones, are common adopters of cloth styles. The smallest and most decorative cloth styles are accepted by congregations that have more contemporary expressions of distinctive dress, such as some Biblical Mennonite Alliance and mainstream Beachy churches. The largest cloth styles are worn by moderate Amish-Mennonite and unaffiliated congregations. Among the moderate Mennonite conferences, the small South Atlantic Mennonite Conference has allowed veils. White veils are used by some missions in Latin America, Africa, Europe, and Australia while black veils are used by some missions in East Asia and North American Indian settlements.

The Mennonite cap style is worn by a variety of Mennonite constituencies. The largest cap styles are worn by women in conservative groups such as the Eastern Pennsylvania Mennonite Church, the Washington-Franklin Mennonite Conference, the Groffdale Conference Mennonite Church (Old Order), and some members of the Weaverland Conference Mennonites and the Nationwide Fellowship Churches. These constituencies have existed apart from the mainstream Mennonite body (MC-USA / MC-Canada) since the 1960s and earlier. The smallest cap styles are worn by those churches most recently separated from or still within mainstream Mennonite bodies, including some of the congregations in Lancaster Conference, Keystone Mennonite, and Biblical Mennonite Alliance. Intermediate-sized coverings are largely worn by constituencies that were established in the 1970s and 1980s, including the Southeastern Mennonite Conference, Midwest Mennonite Fellowship, and Mid-Atlantic Mennonite Fellowship.

Most plainly dressed Brethren congregations have maintained cap style coverings. The most conservative constituencies use a traditional two-piece cap style that covers the ears. Covering strings are often tied under the chin. These constituencies include the horse and buggy-using Old Brethren German Baptist and Old Order German Baptist, and the motor vehicle-using Old German Baptist Brethren and the New Conference Brethren. The Old Order River Brethren use a cap-style covering made of opaque, pliable fabric. The brim is larger and the back piece smaller than the traditional style of the German Baptists. Covering strings are often tied under the chin. The Dunkard Brethren wear a cap style similar to the Beachys and the Mennonites, with or without strings. In essence, it is a smaller version of the German Baptist covering. Various factions have divided from the Church of the Brethren or the Dunkard Brethren and established independent Brethren congregations. These wear a variety of cap styles of a variety of sizes, though several have also permitted veils.

"Note: We are delighted if readers find this section valuable in personal study. Prior to any public use of these next pages, please contact the author."

Amish Style Coverings

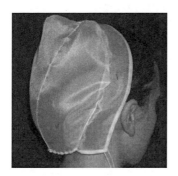

Lancaster (white)

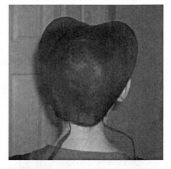

Lancaster (black)

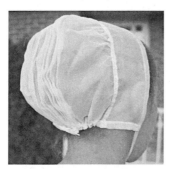

Ontario (Milverton)

Ontario (Aylmer)

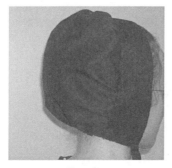

Troyer

Geauga

Daviess (new style)

Daviess (old style)

Elkhart-Lagrange

Unafilliated Orthodox

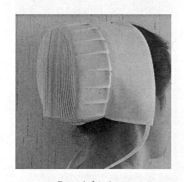

Dan (white)

Dan (black)

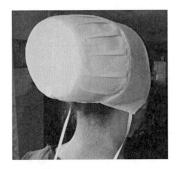

Holmes Co. OO (old style)

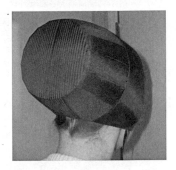

Holmes Co. OO (black)

Holmes Co. OO (white)

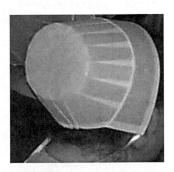

New Order

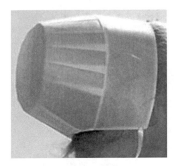

New Order

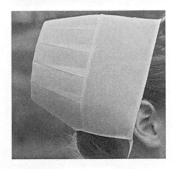

New Order

Amish-Mennonite Style Coverings

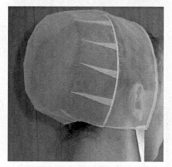

Tampico A-M

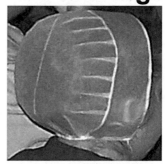

Old Beachy

Bearea A-M (opaque)

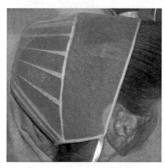

Bearea A-M

Fellowship

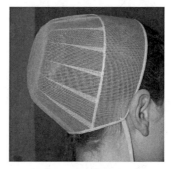

Ambassadors/Maranatha

Ambassadors/Maranatha

Maranatha/Beachy

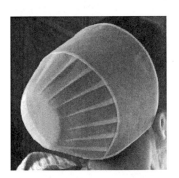

Beachy/Maranatha

Beachy/Maranatha

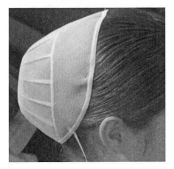

Beachy

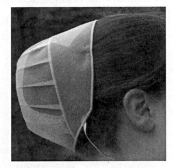

Beachy

Mennonite Style Coverings

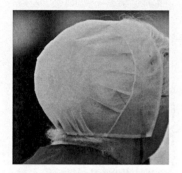

Stauffer

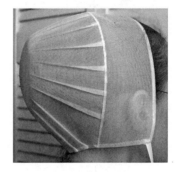

Mennonite Wenger

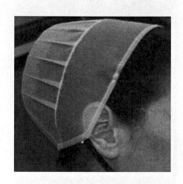

Washington-Franklin

Horning (old style)

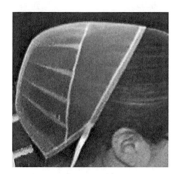

Horning (new style)

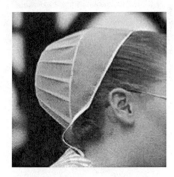

Wisler

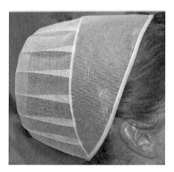

Conservative

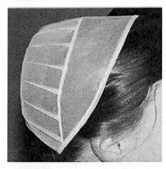

Conservative

Conservative

Conservative Opaque

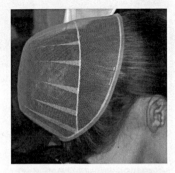

Conservative

Conservative

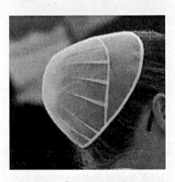

Conservative

Conservative

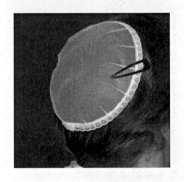

Mainstream

Mainstream

Brethren Style Coverings

River Brethren

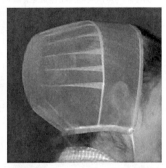

German Baptist

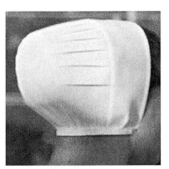

Conservative

Conservative

Dunkard

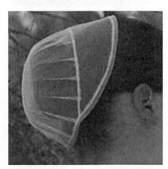

Dunkard

White Veils

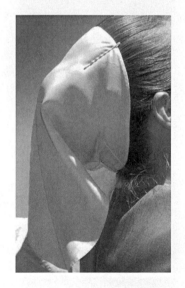

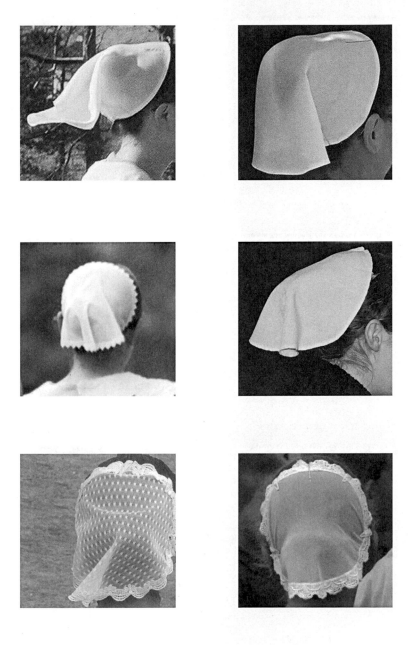

Black Veils

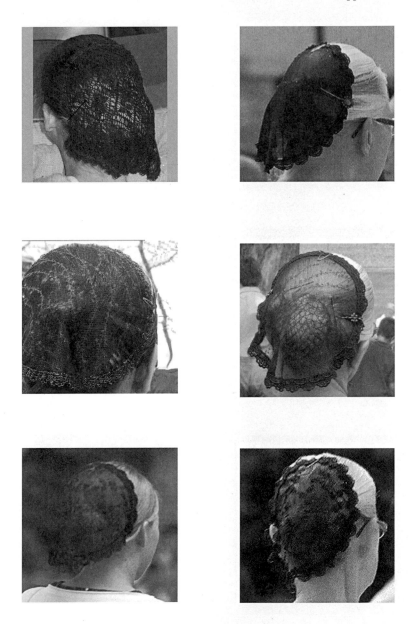

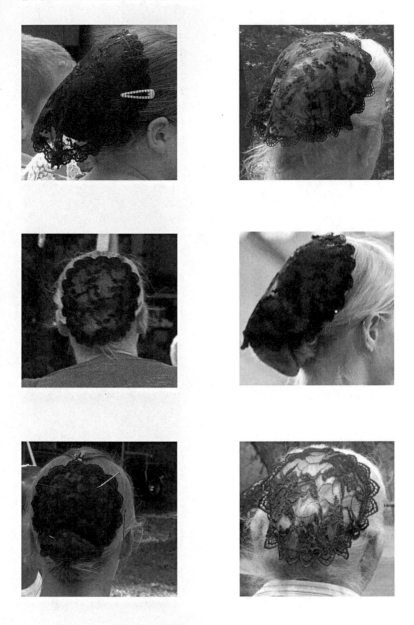

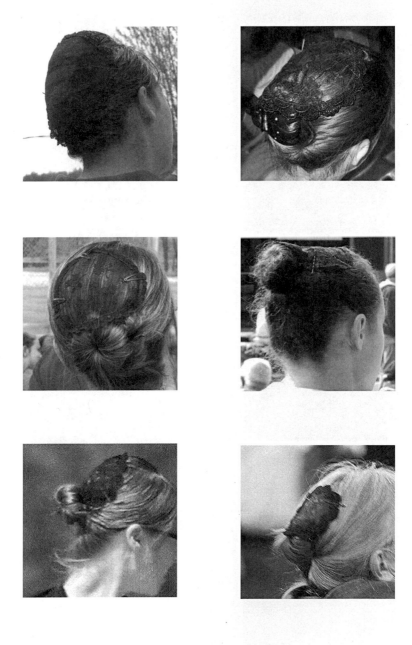

Hutterite Style Coverings

Lehererleut Cap

Lehererleut Outer Scarf

Schmiedeleut Scarf (tied)

Schmiedeleut Scarf (untied)

Miscellaneous Coverings

Holdeman (cap)

Holdeman (scarf)

Apostolic Christian (weekday)

Lancaster Mennonite Conference

Daviess Co. Amish (weekday)

About the Author

Cory Anderson grew up in western Loudoun County, Virginia. He was baptized in 1998 in a Southern Baptist church and began attending a Beachy Amish-Mennonite church in 2002. In 2004 he joined Faith Mission Fellowship, Free Union, Virginia, where he is a member.

He has a bachelor's degree in geography and a master's degree in urban and regional planning. His master's thesis investigated crashes between automobiles and buggies. In 2009 he started work on a Ph.D. in rural sociology at Ohio State University, where he is researching social changes among Anabaptist groups. In addition to his studies, he has worked as a social studies curriculum author and committee member at Christian Light Publications. He and his wife Jennifer presently live in Ohio.